# INDEX

**Numbers in circles on map refer to pages in the text.**

Map, Northern Half of ARIZONA

Map by Reg Manning

## MAP OF SOUTHERN ARIZONA AND CONTINUED INDEX IN BACK OF BOOK

TO RUTH
the girl I met in our
high school art class.

# What Is ARIZONA Really Like ?

by REG·MANNING

CARTOONS BY THE AUTHOR

Reganson
CARTOON BOOKS
PHOENIX, ARIZONA

FIRST EDITION—SEPTEMBER, 1968
Hard cover 3M, Soft cover, 7M

SECOND PRINTING—APRIL, 1969
Soft cover 5M

THIRD PRINTING—JULY, 1970
Soft cover 5M

FOURTH PRINTING — FEBRUARY 1972
Soft cover 5M

FIFTH PRINTING — FEBRUARY 1973
Soft cover 5M

SIXTH PRINTING — FEBRUARY 1974
Soft cover 5M

SEVENTH PRINTING — APRIL 1975
Soft cover 5M

EIGHTH PRINTING — AUGUST 1976
Soft cover 10M

Published by Reganson Cartoon Books
P.O. Box 5242, Phoenix, Arizona 85010

# FOREWORD

Quite frankly, this started out to be a revision of my old "Cartoon Guide of Arizona", published in 1938. That book enjoyed many printings before it got so out of date that I retired it about 15 years ago. I'll confess, a few paragraphs ("Arizona, In Three Bites", and "Recipe For Making Petrified Wood", for instance) are lifted from the old "Guide", but there have been so many changes in this fascinating corner of America, that I found myself forced to write practically a whole new book. Therefore, even "old timers" who have read the old book, should find things in this one that they didn't know before. But it is written primarily for you who may have come to Arizona in recent years, or who may be just visiting here, or who may be planning to come. Or you may be the relative of a proud resident who is sending you this book to brag a little. For each of you I've tried to give honest (though admittedly somewhat biased) answers to the question, "What is Arizona really like?" — in a book compact enough to read in an evening, and light enough to carry along as you travel around.

To cover everything in Arizona would require a library, not one book. So who has time to read a library? But in the space available, these pages will conduct you into every corner of the state — through deserts and forests and canyons — to our National Parks and Recreation Areas, National Monuments (of which Arizona has more than any other state) and Historical Sites. You'll visit scenic marvels and get a backward glimpse into some of Arizona's fascinating history. Towns are mentioned only if they are important crossroads, or seem notable historically. I thought you'd rather hear about points of interest near cities, than about the cities themselves.

If you want to read more about this land, I suggest that you subscribe to "Arizona Highways", the state-owned magazine which is world-famous for its fabulous color photos. And get an official State Road Map (free at state inspection stations, banks, etc.). We claim it is the finest job of highway map making done by any state.

I hope you'll enjoy this book — I know you'll enjoy Arizona.

## WHAT IS ARIZONA REALLY LIKE?

Lots of people think of Arizona as a great expanse of Sahara-like desert, inhabited by gun-toting cowboys, and mebbe a few vanishing Injuns. With scorpions and gila monsters and rattlesnakes 'most everywhere.

Well, Arizona does have deserts, some with sand every color of the rainbow, and some with foliage growing so thick you couldn't ride a horse through it. And with giant saguaro cacti which grow fifty feet high and bloom at night.

But, if you fly over Arizona, you can see pine forests which cover an area twice the size of Massachusetts. There are cowboys in Arizona, some of whom actually herd cattle. And there are Indians, but they're not vanishing — they're increasing like everybody else. There are spots in Arizona where the snow doesn't melt much before June, and other places where the children have seen it only on TV. When a farmer in the dry valleys wants "rain" he orders it sent down from the mountains for a specific date and hour.

As for dangerous critters, your chances of being bitten or stung in Arizona are no greater than anywhere else. But watch out for two-legged varmints driving cars — they're deadly.

## ARIZONA, IN THREE BITES

If you were a giant and wanted to eat the state of Arizona, you would find that, roughly, it would make three large and widely differing mouthfuls.

Starting at the northeast corner (the only point in the United States where four states meet — Utah, Colorado, New Mexico and Arizona)

you would bite out a large quarter circle, sinking your teeth in to encompass the Little Colorado River. This corner takes in the vast Navajo and Hopi Indian Reservations — a wildly beautiful land where prehistoric dinosaurs roamed and left their footprints in the sands — where Indians dwell in picturesque canyons and atop high plateaus. It includes the Painted Desert — eroded bluffs of colored sand and clay following the curve of the Little Colorado in a 150-mile-long "rainbow". And it takes in the famous Petrified Forest.

The second mouthful of your mythical meal would be the "greens" course. Here you would chew off a huge crescent consisting almost entirely of virgin forest — the largest unbroken expanse of Ponderosa pine in America. It would also include, slashing across the northern tip of the crescent, one of the world's great wonders, the Grand Canyon.

The remaining bite would be your dessert — or more properly the desert. Almost all of it, from the Hoover Dam country in the northwest corner, to the Mexican border region on the south, and bordered on the west by Nevada and California, is in the "cactus-belt". It's the portion of Arizona which most folks think of as "typical" — the warm, dry land which travel agents call the "winter playground". Here are great irrigated valleys, and booming cities, where every home is air conditioned, and most of the orange groves have been sub-divided. Not far from modern skyscrapers you can visit Spanish Missions built when America was young.

## ARIZONA CAMEL TRAIL

Whatever route you travel in entering Arizona, you'll be following in somebody's pioneering footsteps — the Spaniards, who came north from Mexico, the Mormons, who came south from Utah, the

forty-niners, the soldiers, the stage lines. When you cross northern Arizona between New Mexico and California, on U.S. Highway 66 and Interstate Highway 40, or on the Santa Fe railway which parallels the route, you'll be following a trail originally surveyed by a camel expedition. This road across rugged terrain, from Ft. Defiance, Arizona westward to Ft. Tejon, California, was selected to test the adaptability of camels for use by the U.S. Army. It was just over a century ago (1856-57) that Congress appropriated $30,000 to import 80 camels from north Africa. They were landed on the gulf coast near San Antonio, Texas, and marched to northern Arizona via El Paso and Albuquerque.

The Army project was put in charge, naturally, of a retired Naval officer, Lt. Edward F. Beale. According to Beale's report to the War Department, the performance of the camels was an unqualified success. A single camel could carry as much as 1000 pounds, and travel twice as far per day as mules could pull wagons. They trod stretches of trail (near San Francisco Peaks) where lava-rock was so sharp other animals couldn't walk without shoes. And they would eat anything, even munching contentedly on the oily leaves of creosote bushes, plants so foul tasting they would gag a goat. The camels swam the Colorado River like water spaniels. Lt. Beale predicted that one day "every mail route across the continent will be conducted and worked altogether with this economic brute."

After reading Lt. Beale's glowing report, the Army asked Congress for authorization to "procure" 1000 more camels. A camel bill was introduced, but immediately ran into stiff opposition from the mule lobby. Meanwhile civilians rushed to speculate on camel transport schemes. One California "camel association" was formed which

never owned a camel. Another syndicate actually imported camels from China. But civilian experience with humped freighting never made any stockholders happy. Americans never seemed to master the art of strapping half a ton of merchandise on a swaying camelback. The load had a way of shaking loose at the most inconvenient moments. And camels could never integrate with mules — one whiff of a camel was enough to stampede a whole mule train. Which did nothing to endear them to established freight line owners.

In 1860 the Civil War broke out and Congress and the Army promptly lost all interest in camels. After the war interest could never be revived. The used camel market hit zero — you couldn't give 'em away. Finally the Army and private owners just turned their herds loose. For years camels roamed wild in Arizona and other western states. Nevada passed a law in 1875 "to prohibit camels and dromedaries from running at large on or about the public highways." Camel hunting became a favorite sport in this region, and 'tis said a principal item of southwest Indian diet for years was — ah — camel soup.

At Quartzsite, in southern Arizona, is a roadside monument to "Hi Jolly" (Hadji Ali), a camel driver imported from north Africa with the first herds. He stayed with the Army till it gave up on camels, then bought a burro and became an Arizona prospector.

## THE NAVAJO INDIANS

Today at Ft. Defiance, site of Arizona's old camel trail terminal, you'll find modern police vehicles instead of dromedaries. It is now the headquarters of the highly efficient reservation police force of the Navajo Indians. Nearby is Window Rock, tribal capital of Navajoland, named after a natural rock formation. They're just north of U.S.

THE OLD -

Hwy. 66 — Interstate Rte. 40, a short drive across the border from Gallup, N.M.

Tourists usually come to Arizona hoping to see some "real live Indians". In this corner of the state you can't miss. The 16 million-acre Navajo reservation completely surrounds the large Hopi Indian reservation, and spreads over the entire northeast part of Arizona and the adjoining northwest corner of New Mexico.

Navajos form the largest Indian tribe in America, and their numbers are increasing. 100 years ago there were barely 10,000 Navajos — today there are more than 70,000. While the tribe is governed by an elected tribal council, which is guiding it in the adoption of many modern ways, the Navajos still speak their own language and retain much of their ancient culture and way of life.

At Window Rock, besides U.S. government and tribal offices, you'll also find the tribal fairgrounds, scene of the great annual fair, staged early in September, and the Navajo civic center, where community events and entertainments are held. Also the Arts and Crafts building, where authentic work of Navajo artisans is displayed and sold the year 'round.

Besides their own police force, the Navajo Indians also have their own courts and judges, empowered to settle disputes and domestic conflicts within the tribe. In judging cases the courts not only consider recorded state law, but give full weight to the centuries-old customs of their people. It is eyebrow lifting to note that lawyers are never allowed in Navajo courts.

-AND NEW

# NAVAJO CUSTOMS AND COSTUMES

In tribal offices, or in nearby towns, you may see Navajo girls in modern dress, but throughout the reservation most Navajo women retain their own distinctive tribal costumes, colorful velveteen blouses, and full, pleated, brightly colored calico skirts. Sometimes they wear three or four skirts at a time. Women do their hair in a roll at the back of the neck, wrapping the middle of the roll neatly and precisely with yarn.

Navajo men also used to wear their hair in a similar knot back of the head, and a few of the "old ones" still do, but most have modern hair cuts and, in common with most southwest Indians, have adopted the traditional style of the cowboy, complete with ten gallon hat, often uncreased. And, yes, high-heel cowboy boots are replacing moccasins.

A Navajo never dies in the house if anyone can prevent it. When a member of the family gets so sick that death seems probable, he is taken outdoors to die. For the Navajo has abject fear of Death with a capital "D". If anyone dies in a dwelling, that place is cursed, he believes, and no Navajo will ever willingly enter it again.

Less grim is the custom relating to mothers-in-law. A husband must never, never meet his wife's mom face to face. Penalty for breaking this rule, they say (and who can deny?) is a lot of tough luck for both parties. Consequently, when mother-in-law comes to visit, hubby takes off to call on friends.

Among Navajos, as with some other tribes, divorce is simple. If a husband comes home and finds his personal belongings set outside the door, he knows his marriage is finished.

# THE NAVAJO AT HOME

A Navajo wife never has to hear, "Now this is bizness, dear, you wouldn't understand." Among this people the women are the "business men". They own the greatest flocks of sheep, and they do their own dickering with the traders for sale of the wool. They are nearly always more wealthy than the men. But, it must be noted, women and girls also do the physical work of caring for their flocks.

The Navajo is several centuries ahead of the trailer tourist. Instead of towing around a "mobile home" his ancient practice has been to set up a dwelling at each new stopping place, a one-room, circular hut, with domed roof and ceiling, called a hogan (HOE-gahn). It is constructed of materials at hand, logs, or rocks, plastered with mud. The single door is always on the east side, opening toward the rising sun. The hogan is furnished with a true antique-style chair-divan-bed combination — a sheepskin spread on the floor. A fireplace or small stove occupies the center of the room. An opening in the dome of the ceiling will let the smoke out if a stovepipe hasn't been rigged up.

Today many Navajo families have small "modern" rectangular houses, but it's doubtful if the hogan will ever be entirely abandoned by the Indians following their herds in constant search for grass in the vast arid reservation.

Of course, with the coming of good highways, regular trailers are coming into use among the Navajos, along with all kinds of autos. Nearly every family, it seems, owns a pickup truck, which does double duty as a utility and pleasure vehicle. A pickup will haul an entire family, near or far, to various tribal functions.

# NAVAJO ARTS AND CRAFTS

Navajo blankets, perhaps more accurately called rugs, are famous the world over. Women of the tribe practically grow these beautiful works of art. Not only do they raise the sheep, they clip the wool, card and dye it, spin it into yarn and weave it on their looms. They even build the looms. A Navajo weaver makes up designs for a blanket "out of her own head" as she goes along.

Incidentally, the bright colored wrap you may see around a Navajo's shoulders will not be a Navajo blanket. It is a "Pendleton" blanket purchased at a store. It serves all practical purposes, and the Indian can buy several of them for the price obtained for one home-grown Navajo blanket.

On the other hand, jewelry worn by a Navajo is always genuine "Navajo jewelry". In fact, the amount of jewelry owned and worn on the reservation is a measure of "status". The men of the tribe are the silversmiths who fashion truly distinctive necklaces, bracelets and concho-belts, studded with native turquoise.

Navajo sandpainting is just what the name says, pictures made with sand. This art, which, like rug weaving, may often be seen demonstrated at Northern Arizona and New Mexico fairs and expositions, is actually a religious rite, used in healing. The "artists" are medicine men, whose art has been passed from generation to generation. With unbelievable skill they "draw" intricate designs by letting black or brightly colored sand pour from an opening in their fingers. Every color, every line is part of a symbolic pattern, as precise as if drawn with brush or pen. In the evening of the same day it was created, a sandpainting which has taken hours to complete will be completely wiped out before the sun sets. That's part of the ritual, to erase the evil spirits.

# THE HOPI INDIAN VILLAGES

Have you ever day-dreamed about going back a thousand years in history to see how people lived? Less than two hours, via paved roads, north of Holbrook and Winslow life goes on today in the Hopi (HOPE-ee) villages much as it did centuries ago. When Columbus was a boy at least one of these villages, Old Oraibi, was 500 years old. It is still there, built of the same stone, occupying the identical real estate. Several of the other villages are at least two or three centuries old.

The Hopi reservation, as we've mentioned, is completely surrounded by that of the Navajos. Nine Hopi towns are built atop three high mesas, or plateaus, the steep walls of which rise hundreds of feet above the surrounding plain. The lofty sites were originally chosen as protection against the Navajos and Apaches, who were not exactly the best of neighbors in those times. Though danger of attack has long since passed, Hopis refuse to abandon the sky-high homes of their fathers — or more accurately, of their mothers, since mom does most maintenance work on the stone house, and it's looked upon as her home.

The Hopi villages, three to each mesa, are pueblos — literally "apartment houses" constructed of stone with mud mortar, two or three stories high. Each family builds and owns its own apartment. Today as in ancient times, all water must be carried or hauled up the cliffs to the villages, from springs far below. (Before you drive into the Indian reservations fill your canteens with water. It is a scarce item in this part of the country.)

# POTTERY, BASKETS AND KACHINAS

Hopi Indians are great artists. The women make beautiful baskets, and their pottery is unexcelled in America. Women of each mesa have their own particular craft, not practiced in the villages of the other

HOPI
KACHINA
DOLL
MAKER

SUN
FRIENDSHIP
STARS
— SOME HOPI SYMBOLS
USED ON KACHINAS —
LIGHTNING
CLOUDS
RAIN

mesas. The famous decorated Hopi pottery is made exclusively on First Mesa, while fine coiled basketwork is done on Second Mesa. On Third Mesa an entirely different, brightly colored, wicker basketry is performed.

Men are the weavers of the Hopi people. The finest garments worn by women of the tribe at ceremonials are done by these men, who also weave kilts, belts and blankets which are part of costumes worn in Hopi dances.

Beautiful ceremonial dances are staged by various clans throughout the year. Each clan has its own kiva (KEE-va), or "club room", where the men go to sing, talk, practice their rituals and just get away from the women. (Just like in white man's lodges.) Whenever you see a ladder protruding from a square hole in the center of a village plaza, that will be a kiva entrance, to the "club room" which is built underground, along the general lines of a Kansas cyclone cellar.

Kachina dances, performed at unpredictable intervals, December through July, are particularly interesting to watch, because of the elaborate masks and costumes of the performers. Each represents one of the gods believed to control various phases of Hopi life. Kachina dolls, skillfully carved from cottonwood roots, and painted by Hopi men, are careful replicas of Kachina dancers, accurate to the last detail. The dolls are given to children as part of their religious training.

## THEY DANCE WITH SNAKES

Most spectacular of all North American Indian rites is the famous Hopi Snake Dance, held in various of the villages the latter part of August. The dancers really carry deadly rattlesnakes in their mouths; as each completes dancing 'round the square, he drops the snake in

a circle of corn meal on the ground, where the "gatherer" calmly retrieves it. (We saw one gatherer with both hands so full of rattlers that they became tangled, so he dumped them on the ground, combed them straight with his fingers, then picked them up again before they could escape into the startled crowd. Which may explain why most spectators prefer to purchase space above the arena on steps or roofs of houses.) Hopis do not drug rattlesnakes, do not pull their fangs nor remove venom sacs. They just know how to handle the reptiles, gently and fearlessly. Sometimes they are bitten, but they never miss a step nor show any concern.

The Snake Dance is a supplication for rain, and, after the ceremony the snakes are carried away and released, to carry the message to the gods underground. The reptiles evidently make the trip at supersonic speed, because spectators of the ritual seldom get off the reservation without being drenched.

Never take your camera to the Snake Dance — leave it in your car. This is a most sacred religious rite and Hopis strictly prohibit taking pictures.

Practically every act of Hopi life is marked by some ceremony. Feathers play a great part in the religious scheme of things. "Prayer feathers", the down from eagles' breasts, which will float out of the hand when a prayer is whispered over them, may be seen everywhere; in doorways, tied to kiva ladders, adorning kachina dolls. Nearly every Hopi has one tied somewhere in his hair.

## GIANT ECONOMY SIZED CORNFLAKES

Hopis could probably lay claim to invention of the cornflake. Certainly they make the largest "flakes" we've ever seen. For that's what their native bread, called "piki" (pee-kee) really is — a huge cornflake, rolled into a tight scroll. The Hopi housewife, using corn from the fam-

PIKI ROLL

ily fields, grinds the flour herself by hand, on a stone "metate" (may-TAH-tay), then whips up her batter, adding pink, blue or lemon-yellow coloring. Her oven is also stone, worn glass-smooth. On its slick, heated surface, she spreads the batter with deft, rapid strokes of her hand. The cooked, colored flake is lifted and, while still moist, is rolled for convenient munching.

Corn for piki bread is grown under conditions which would make any but a Hopi farmer sob with despair. The cornfields look pitiful, with stalks scarcely arm-pit high — but they produce a fine crop of ears. And Hopi corn is grown in "living color" — the kernels may be bright red, blue, snow white or varicolored — so beautiful the ears are prized as wall decorations in homes of the Southwest. The Hopi farmers also produce excellent harvests of melons, beans, peppers, apricots and peaches.

There is one Hopi village, not on the mesa, where farming conditions are more favorable. Sometime in the 1800's Indians from Old Oraibi founded the "modern" pueblo of Moenkopi to be a sort of agricultural outpost, located on the banks of a wash, making irrigation possible. It's about 40 miles west of Oraibi mesa, near the old trading post of Tuba City, but it is only two miles from U.S. Hwy. 164, which makes it the most accessible of all Hopi settlements.

## CANYON DE CHELLY

Before the Hopis or Navajos came to this corner of Arizona it was inhabited by cliff dwellers, whose abandoned, but well preserved habitations may be seen in several National Monuments. One Monument where you can see prehistoric cliff dwellings by the score is Canyon de Chelly (pronounced day-SHAY). It is actually made up of three main canyons, which join at the west in a common mouth and fan out to the east in a sort of gigantic "turkey track", with toe prints 15 miles

long. The canyons are deep crevices in brilliant red sandstone, the walls of which are higher than the Empire State building at their deepest points. In places the sand floor which separates these sheer walls seems little wider than a broad highway, and almost as smooth. Driving on this "road" in an ordinary car, however, would be risky, since it can become like quicksand when wet, and almost as bad when too dry.

Wind and water have hollowed out numerous caves in the cliffs, and in almost every such niche is a prehistoric ruin. Some are small buildings, while others are so large they look like medieval castles. You'll find it hard to imagine how ancient builders ever reached some of the cliff sites, hundreds of feet straight up, let alone getting building materials up there.

Only a few miles from the mouth of the gorge is the White House, most accessible and most beautiful of all the cliff dwellings. Its name doesn't result from any resemblance to the President's home, but from the fact that it is plastered chalky white, a plaster job that has lasted for centuries.

One of the three main canyons, Monument Canyon, is named for the spectacular 800-foot high monolith, called "Spider Rock". It looks very much like a full sized New York skyscraper, carved from solid rock.

## BLOOD AND SANDSTONE

The United States has been in existence as a nation almost 200 years. It has been estimated that the prehistoric cliff dwellers occupied Canyon de Chelly at least five times that long, which impressively testifies to its fortress like qualities. In 1692 the Navajo Indians, retreating before the advancing Spanish conquest, moved into the abandoned canyon and thereafter it became their almost impregnable stronghold. A Spanish raiding party did slip into the gorge in 1804 and massacred

SPIDER ROCK

REG 82

women, children and old men they found hiding in a cave. Punishment was swift, however, for pursuing Navajo warriors caught and killed all but a few of the raiders. They named the scene of the massacre Canyon del Muerto — Canyon of Death.

In the winter of 1863 the cliff-walled fortress became a trap where U. S. troops, under command of famed Kit Carson, cornered and captured most of the Navajo tribe — 7000 half-starved Indians. In a "gov'ment experiment" that failed, the captives were moved en masse to the Bosque Redondo, a sort of concentration camp reservation on the Pecos river in eastern New Mexico. But the proud Navajos were so discontented in the new surroundings that they were finally permitted to return to their beloved land of colored sands.

Though Canyon de Chelly is now a National Monument, many Navajo families still live there, farming the sandy soil, and raising sheep. Once in a while Hopi Indians make trips to the canyon to trap eaglets among the crags. These are taken back to their villages and tethered to the housetops to provide a living supply of ceremonial feathers.

Monument headquarters is located at the little town of Chinle (chin-lee — Indian name, not Chinese). Accommodations and horses are available, and canyon trips in special cars may be arranged.

## THE TRADING POST

One phase of frontier America still exists today. In more remote parts of the Navajo reservation you will find Indian trading posts where barter is carried on much as it was in pioneer days, though such modern innovations as laundromats, coke machines and gas pumps allow more and more posts to compete with the supermarkets of nearby towns.

Time was when the trading post was the Indian's only commer-

DON LORENZO, TRADER

cial link with the white man's world. The trader was more than just a trader. He was often the Indian's advisor, doctor, pawnbroker, interpreter and trusted friend. Such a trader was John "Don" Lorenzo Hubbell. At Ganado, 37 miles south of Canyon de Chelly, 54 miles west of Gallup, you may visit the Hubbell Trading Post, founded in 1876 by Don Lorenzo and operated by the Hubbells for 90 years. Today it is a National Historic Site — not a "reconstruction", but the actual trading post, home and grounds acquired intact from the Hubbell family by the National Park Service.

You may inspect the Hubbell home, see the collection of Navajo rugs, the ceilings covered with Indian baskets, and walls lined with paintings given to Don Lorenzo by artists who enjoyed his hospitality. Throughout the years hundreds of famous people, including President Teddy Roosevelt, were guests in this fabulous house.

The post itself is still "live" — they have a trader to carry on active trading with the Don's old friends, the Indians. We once sat in on such a trading session between one of Lorenzo's sons and a Navajo family — the weighing of wool — the friendly pow-wow in the trader's office (in Navajo language) with all the family taking part (each owned some of the sheep) — the oldest woman puffing a long cigar with dignity — when she spoke, all listened (she owned the most sheep) — finally the family filing into the store to select merchandise.

# RAINBOWS ON THE GROUND

Nature can teach the Indian sand painters a thing of two. It has "sand-painted" the southern border of the Navajo-Hopi country — a 150-mile semi-circle following the north side of the Little Colorado River called the Painted Desert. In fact this is actually the area from which Indians have always obtained the colored pigments for their brilliant sand paintings.

Quite a few million years ago, this country was the floor of the ocean. Successive layers of sediment were stained or dyed by the mineral laden waters. Then the ground slowly lifted and the water drained off. Erosion chewed out great gullies, exposing vari-colored cross sections of cliffs and filling stream beds with sands of every hue. The result is a wild land of mounds and bluffs that looks like someone had gathered all the rainbows from the sky, boiled 'em like spaghetti, then spilled the whole kettle full all over the desert.

The choicest views of the Painted Desert are in Petrified Forest National Park, which may be seen on a short but spectacular scenic drive north of U.S. 66-Interstate 40. There are a series of viewpoints that will tax your color film and leave you breathless.

At times, in certain light, wind stirs the colored sands so land and sky seem to merge in a glowing fantasy. They are thinking of exporting some of the dust to Hollywood — then they can have smog in Technicolor.

Besides Indians, this wild blue (and red and yellow ocre and mauve) yonder is inhabited by wild horses, descendants perhaps of the animals which used to be corraled at the old Pony Express station which operated out there in 1880. However, there is no truth to the story that this is where TV westerns get all their horses called, "Old Paint."

## NO PLACE FOR WHITTLERS

Besides the Painted Desert, there are six distinct "forests" within the 141 square miles of Petrified Forest National Park. But you're a couple of million years too late to find any wood, or shade, among the thousands of trees. For, as the name of the Park has tipped you

FOREST FIRES ARE NO PROBLEM IN *THIS* FOREST!

off, all the trees here have turned to stone. And the trees are really logs, and they're all lying down. But any disappointment you may have will disappear when you see the beauty of the stone woods. Each of the six forests has its individual characteristics and color scheme. The petrified logs, usually broken into short lengths, display every shade of the spectrum, reds predominating. The ground is carpeted with jewel-like fragments, but no visitor is allowed to pick up and take away "even just one teensy bit." (Lucky for you this rule was put into force. Otherwise the millions of visitors throughout the years would have left nothing for you to see.)

There are a few long logs which have withstood the natural forces (earthquakes, maybe?) that fractured so many of the others, and these are each in-one-piece. A famous one is "Old Faithful", located in Rainbow Forest near the park museum. It was once a giant of the forest, and its base end, with the evidences of broken-off roots, is a favorite background for photo snappers. Most noted tree of all is "Agate Bridge", a 111-foot-long stone trunk which spans an arroyo 44 feet wide. It is eight miles from the Park headquarters, three miles from Second Forest. All these trees were once normal living, wooden trees, related to pines and redwoods. Some even show evidences of scars from prehistoric forest fires, one problem which never worries this forest today.

The Petrified Forest National Park, 19 miles east of Holbrook, may be entered from either U.S. 66 or U.S. 206 — it's wedged between the highways, except for the Painted Desert drive north of 66. The Park museum, near the south entrance, is a "must see" attraction in its own right. Here the park naturalist explains the fossilized remains of strange

THOUSANDS OF TREES — BUT NOT A SPECK O' SHADE!

critters and plants which lived here when it was a vast swamp. You'll see the finest exhibit of petrified wood in the world, an outstanding item of which is a perfect six-inch sphere — a great jewel, hand ground in Germany from the almost diamond-hard "wood".

A point of special interest in the Park is Newspaper Rock, which is covered with pictures chipped in stone by prehistoric newsmen. These ancient etchings are not the "comic pages" of a bygone age — all stories in that time had to be told in pictures because nobody had learned to write. Which was just as well, since none of the subscribers could read.

The old argument of pen vs sword had evidently already started, for we find that stone-writers' etching tools were made of chips of petrified wood — and arrowheads of their warriors were made of the same material.

There are more than a hundred prehistoric ruins in the National Park, most of them constructed of petrified wood . . . antediluvian log cabins.

## RECIPE FOR MAKING PETRIFIED WOOD

Question number one about the Petrified Forest is always, "How can wood turn to stone?" The answer is really quite simple. We'll give you the formula, and you can try it out in your own kitchen. When you've got lots of time. Here it is:

Take one tree and immerse it in water; stir gently till it becomes waterlogged and sinks to the bottom of the pan; stir in generous quantities of silica, manganese, aluminum, copper, lithium, carbon, and for coloring, add iron as desired. Now pour in a layer of sediment about 3000 ft. deep; allow the mixture to settle for a couple of million years,

then gradually, during a few million more years, drain off the water (you can't rush this). Set out to dry in a strong breeze. When the wind has blown away the 3000-ft. layer, you will find that the minerals have soaked into the trees, replacing the cell structure of wood with stone.

Money back if it doesn't work.

# A STAR FELL IN ARIZONA

Ever wonder, as you watched a shooting star, "what if one of those babies should smack into the earth head on?" Not far from Arizona's Petrified Forest that's exactly what happened. About 50,000 years ago (scientists guess) a huge meteor came whistling in from the north over Grand Canyon and plowed into the ground 20 miles west of Winslow. Fortunately Winslow was not there at the time. Today you can drive five miles south of U.S. 66-Interstate 40 and see the hole it made, Meteor Crater.

Throw a rock into smooth mud and it will make a hole with puckered edges. Magnify that hole in your mind's eye till it measures almost a mile from rim to rim (4150 feet to be exact) by 570 feet deep, and you will get a pretty good idea of what Meteor Crater looks like from the air. Only it is gouged out of solid rock instead of mud. The "pucker" raises its rim 150 feet above the surrounding plain. The meteorite came in at an angle and buried itself some 1500 feet below the original ground level, beneath the south rim.

Tons of meteor fragments, large and small, have been collected around the crater. Judging from drillings and scientific surveys of the great mass of metalic materials still underground, the molten chunk of iron and nickel which crash landed here must have been equivalent to a metal ball 500 feet thick, weighing at least three million tons.

The crater is privately owned, but the charge for looking into it is reasonable, and there is a museum with many interesting displays, lectures, etc. You can hike into the crater if you're ambitious. As you stand on the rim and gaze into this gigantic splash, a fascinating idea forces itself into your consciousness. What if the body which crashed here was not an ordinary meteor? What if some craft from outer space tried to make a soft landing, and . . . .

## SAN FRANCISCO PEAKS

On the horizon, west of Meteor Crater, is "God's Country". Lots of people use that designation for their favorite section of the country, but the only place we know of which can document its claim to the title is San Francisco Peaks in northern Arizona. The Hopi Indians will solemnly testify that the peaks are the home of their sacred Kachina Gods. Every spring, they say, the Kachinas come out of the mountains when they hear the chants of ceremonial dances in the villages, to receive the homage of their people.

By more mundane standards the three San Francisco Peaks still reach the heavens. The loftiest, Humphreys Peak, is almost 13,000 feet above sea level, which makes it the high spot of Arizona scenery. The other two peaks, only a few hundred feet less in altitude, are Agassiz and Fremont. Botanists are fascinated by the fact that, from the top of the peaks to the bottom of Grand Canyon, a very small area by their standards, they can find plants of every climatic zone from arctic to sub-tropic.

At one time the San Francisco Peaks were a good deal higher, till they blew their tops in a blaze of fireworks, for they are the highest of 400 old volcanoes located in this region. The last eruption happened

SAN FRANCISCO PEAKS

almost exactly 1000 years ago — you could say the ground had hardly stopped smoking when the Spaniards arrived in America.

High on the slopes of Mount Agassiz is one of the state's most popular ski resorts, Arizona Snow Bowl, only a short drive from Flagstaff, where all kinds of accommodations are ample.

# THE JULY 4TH CITY

In the summer of 1876 a party of pioneers was camped by a big spring near the foot of San Francisco Peaks, along the trail surveyed earlier by the army camel corps. The 100th anniversary of Independence Day was coming up, and they wanted to celebrate. There wasn't a firecracker in camp, nor any nearby post office selling "centennial stamps", but one thing they could do, and that was to fly the flag in the grandest manner possible. They selected the tallest pine they could find, stripped it of branches and bark, and fastened Old Glory to the lofty staff with rawhide thongs.

The great bare pine became a landmark, famed by travelers from Sante Fe to San Francisco. So it was that the town of Flagstaff had a well established name before it even became a town.

July 4th is still the biggest day of the year for Flagstaff visitors. The city's "birthday" is celebrated with its famous Indian Pow Wow, an all-Indian festival, lasting three days, with thousands of Indians from many tribes participating in afternoon rodeos and evening ceremonials, and camping at night among the pines.

With the coming of the railroad in 1882, Flagstaff became a roaring rail and lumber center, supplying ties and bridge timbers to the road. Its wild and wooly history, as yet untapped by the TV writers, rivals that of any town in the west. In those early days, a labor prob-

lem could be as dangerous as a cattle war. For instance, take the time that a certain contractor was late getting the money to meet his payroll. The "grievance committee" hung 'im.

## THEY DISCOVERED A SPECK

If you are planning a trip to Mars (and in this day and age you might just be) don't fail to visit Lowell Observatory in Flagstaff. They have what is probably the best display of Martian globes and road (or rather, canal) maps in existence. The observatory is renowned for its discovery of Planet "X" (no relation to Brand "X") which was later named Pluto. You can see the original photographic plate on which this heavenly body made its debut before the camera. To the layman a snapshot negative of the stars looks like nothing so much as a piece of film covered with fly specks. One day in 1930 the astronomers found a speck out of place on one of the plates they had just exposed. As soon as they determined that it was not the work of a subversive fly, they knew they had made the great discovery.

The Museum of Northern Arizona is another attraction in Flagstaff which you should not miss. Its fascinating displays of pottery and artifacts, prehistoric through modern, are so arranged that you can trace the story of man's centuries of sojourn in Arizona. And dioramas are used to let you see how Arizona's scrambled landscape got that way. You'll see the skeleton of a prehistoric reptile and sandstone slabs with the actual tracks he left as he strolled near here. At times Indian artisans appear in person at the museum to demonstrate their crafts.

The campus of Northern Arizona University, one of the state's three major brain factories, is located in Flagstaff.

Very few regions on earth can compare with the environs of Flagstaff in the number and variety of tourist attractions. Besides the Grand Canyon, Painted Desert, Indian country and Meteor Crater, all within sight of San Francisco Peaks, there are canyons, lava flows, ice caves, and prehistoric dwellings close by.

# THE RUINED RUINS

Walnut Canyon, only nine miles from Flagstaff, is a National Monument which is a graphic example of what other prehistoric dwelling places would be like if National Monuments had never been created. By the time this Monument had been established in 1915 several decades of vandals had enjoyed free and easy access to the 300 ancient ruins which filled niches of the beautiful canyon. "Pot hunters", finding that small doors did not let in enough light for them to search for artifacts, simply tumbled the walls into the canyon. And, of course, they carried away every object of interest they could find.

Fortunately, enough of the ruins remain to make Walnut Canyon well worth visiting, particularly since they are so very close to Flagstaff. Even where the walls have been destroyed, you can clearly trace the outlines of the rooms. All along the ledges prehistoric lampblack from thousands of prehistoric campfires still blackens the rock. Ceilings were formed by low roofs of the caves, so there was not room to build multiple storied apartments. Each dwelling was apparently occupied by a separate family.

In Walnut Canyon walls you'll notice a stratum of white rock. This is Kaibab limestone, the same "white streak" which may be seen at the rim of Grand Canyon, 60 miles north of here. Some 80 species of fossils of sea life have been found in the limestone, indicating that it was once below the ocean. Today it is about 6500 feet above sea level. Even in geology, looks like everything is going up.

# PERPETUAL GLOW OF EVENING

The first time you see it, you get the feeling that something is wrong. You can't tell why — it's an exceptionally symmetrical volcanic cone, with the orange-red rays of the setting sun painting the rim in brilliant contrast to the smoke-black slopes lower down — nothing strange about that. But there's something that just isn't right. Then

you glance at your watch — and back at that red rim — and now you get it. The sun will not be setting for hours — the sunset coloring of the crater's rim can't be caused by the sun's evening rays. The answer is ash, red sulphur-stained cinders spilled all around the lip of the cone. That's what gives Sunset Crater National Monument its perpetual lighting effect, and its name. At any time of day, cloudy or fair, it seems to be bathed in the last golden rays of sundown.

It was in the fall of the year 1064 AD that molten lava suddenly spewed from the ground through a "volcanic vent", while thousands of tons of cinders and ash billowed high in the air. Heavier material fell back around the vent and rapidly built up the 1000-foot-high cone which is Sunset Crater. The precise dating of the event was established by study of tree rings in trees living at the time of the eruption, and covered by the ash.

To reach the National Monument you drive about 10 miles north of Flagstaff on U.S. 89, and turn off four miles via paved road. Alongside this road, winding through the pines is a jet black river — a river turned to stone. It is Bonito Lava Flow, which a few hundred years ago was a boiling river of melted rock, flowing from the base of the crater on its way to the canyon of the Little Colorado River. The jagged waves are still so sharp you almost feel they could be warm, but near the crater there is a cave in the lava which contains ice the year 'round.

## BUILT ON ASHES

The eruption of Sunset Crater in 1064, which covered 800 square miles of land with a thick layer of volcanic ash, undoubtedly scared the living daylights out of the local inhabitants. But, far from driving out all the people, it actually caused a great land rush into the region. The Indians discovered that the cinder blanket acted as moisture

retaining mulch, and turned the whole area into excellent farm land. As news of the agricultural bonanza spread, Indians started moving in from all directions, first by dozens, then by the hundreds, until during the next century the area north of Sunset Crater was dotted with villages and farms. It's estimated that the "metropolitan" population reached 8000.

One of the largest towns was the pueblo of Wupatki (woo-POT-key). The ruins of Wupatki are still there, preserved in the National Monument of the same name, about 11 miles north of Sunset Crater. It's reached by paved highway, 13 miles east of a well-marked turnoff on U.S. 89. Wupatki, which had a population of 300 (CofC estimate) in the year 1200 A.D., stood three stories high and had about 100 rooms. Even in its present condition it is spectacular, its red sandstone masonry fitted into the rocks of the ledge, and utilizing the solid stone to form the walls of rooms wherever possible. At Wupatki you'll see one feature never discovered at any other pueblo, ancient or modern. It is a large circle, 53 feet across, smoothed out of a natural rock platform near the ruin, with a low stone wall all around. It was probably a ceremonial dance floor.

Tree ring studies show there was a drouth which started about 1215, and lasted throughout the century. Everything dried up and winds blew away the cinders in black "dust-bowl" clouds. As farms blew away, so did the people. By 1300 A.D. Wupatki and its sister villages had become ghost towns.

## THE CLIFF CITIES

Less than 100 miles northeast of Wupatki, and about four centuries after it was abandoned, a Spanish tourist scrambled up the side of Nitsin Canyon to a large, beautiful cliff dwelling, and true to the tradition of tourists of every era, scratched his name in the clay plaster

WUPATKI

on a wall in one of the many rooms: "S-hapeiro Ano Dom 1661". Senor S-hapeiro found the ruin looking very much the same in 1661 as it does today. It was not visited again by white men until 1909, when it was discovered by Dr. Byron Cummings and John Wetherill, who also located two other marvelous cliff cities nearby. (see also Page 33). The very same year all three were included in a preserve called Navajo National Monument, before vandals or thoughtless visitors could get to them. Which accounts for their remarkable state of preservation. The Indians, of course, throughout the centuries never dreamt of disturbing the "dead" dwellings.

The place S-hapeiro autographed is now known as Inscription House Ruin. To reach it you'll have to scramble like the Spaniard did, two miles (and half a day) by foot trail from your auto. And don't forget to take your canteen.

The other two ruins, Betatakin ("hillside house") and Keet Seel ("broken pottery") are bigger, and if possible, even more perfectly preserved than Inscription House. And Betatakin is reached by a paved road only 15 miles north of U.S. 164. It is a large pueblo, with 60 living rooms and as many smaller rooms, used for storage, corn grinding and other purposes. There are half a dozen ceremonial kivas. The great structure is built within the half-dome of an enormous symmetrical cave 235 feet high at the arch, and 135 feet deep. You get a breathtaking view of the ruin across the canyon at Sandal Point, from which a new trail gives access to guided tours into the cliff city.

Keet Seel is largest of the three, built in a cave longer than a football field, with more than 200 rooms. It is also the least accessible of the ruins, reached via an 11-mile trail. The place gives you the feeling that it was only recently abandoned. You half expect to hear the cries

of retreating former inhabitants echoing down the canyon. Prehistoric corncobs lie on the floor where occupants left them. Pottery and corn grinders were scattered about, probably too bulky to carry away.

# THE NAVAJO TRAIL

Cameron, a picturesque cluster of buildings — rambling trading post, hotel-motel, domed Navajo hogans, service station — perched on the brink of the Little Colôrado River gorge, is a highway hub, with every spoke leading to a scenic wonderland. Southward 68 miles on U.S. 89 is Flagstaff; north, same distance, same highway, is Glen Canyon Dam and Lake Powell; to the west a mere 32 miles on Rte. 64 is the Grand Canyon; 75 miles eastward via Rte. 264 are the Hopi villages. And to the northeast the "Navajo Trail", U.S. 164, stretches 175 miles through the reservation, past turnoffs to Navajo National Monument, and Monument Valley, to the Four Corners, where Arizona meets its three sister states.

The trail actually starts at the road junction 17 miles north of Cameron. A dozen miles from this "Y", near the Hopi town of Moenkopi (see page 12) is old Tuba City, with its trading post, founded in 1870. Here is Western Headquarters of Navajo tribal activities, with community center, police complex, schools and hospitals. Tall poplar trees tell you this was once a Mormon settlement — poplars were the "trademark" of pioneers from Utah, planted wherever they explored.

Half an hour's drive from Tuba City is Tonalea, with another old trading post and, nearby, a famous landmark, the Elephant's Feet. Here nature started to sculp a colossal Republican mascot in sandstone, but gave up after finishing the two front legs, ankle high. Too bad, because even this small part of the elephant's anatomy is 70 feet high — the complete statue would have been big enough to suit even Barry Goldwater.

THE ELEPHANT'S FEET

28

Six miles past Tonalea you can turn north to Inscription House Ruin, or 53 miles away to Navajo Mountain Trading Post, where pack trips can be arranged to Rainbow Bridge. (See page 33). Until Glen Canyon Dam was built, this breathtaking trail ride was the only way to reach the famous stone arch. 31 miles from Tonalea is the turnoff to Betatakin Ruin — Navajo Nat'l Monument.

# MONUMENT VALLEY AND THE FOUR CORNERS

Kayenta, 83 miles from Cameron, was founded as a trading post by John Wetherill in 1909, before there were any roads at all. Today it's an important crossroads, the junction point of U.S. 164 and paved Rte. 464 to Monument Valley and scenic southeast Utah. Monument Valley, straddling the Arizona-Utah line, is an architect's dream turned to stone, life-size. Here Nature has carved out a skyline on the lonely Navajo horizon, with spires, castles and skyscrapers, that would be the envy of any great metropolis.

Since the movie classic, "Stagecoach", was filmed in Monument Valley in 1938 (you must have seen it on the "late show") this has become a favorite Hollywood "location". But not even wide screen and full color can quite prepare you for the vast vistas of the real landscape. A Navajo Tribal Park, part of an extensive program being developed to serve tourists on the reservation, has been established at the Valley, with a visitor observation center and a 14-mile drive (small fee). Special guided tours, off the pavement into the Valley, are available at Kayenta and at Goulding's Trading Post and Lodge near the Park entrance. They're well worth it — guides who speak the Navajo language will take you to visit hogans of the Indians, who are as colorful as their background.

When you return to Kayenta and resume your trip along U.S. 164, you'll probably be all out of adjectives and color film, but another

unique experience awaits you 80 miles away at the Four Corners. There on the ground is a slab of concrete, 24 feet square, divided into four equal sections, marked with the names and bronze state seals of Arizona, New Mexico, Colorado and Utah. At the center of this monument is the only spot in America where four states touch. You can circle the square in your car, touring all the states in a matter of seconds, or you can get out and actually stand in the several states at once.

# GRAND CANYON CROSSINGS

In the year 1540, Hopi Indians told the Spaniards some pretty wild tales about a Grand Canyon to the north. So Capt. Lopez de Cardenas and 25 of his men took a jaunt up to have a look. After two or three days of trying unsuccessfully to scramble down to the Colorado River, the captain was overcome by a spirit of generosity — he decided to let someone else have the honor of crossing the river first. It was 236 years later, about two months before George Washington crossed the Delaware, until anyone crossed the Colorado — two Spanish padres, named Escalante and Dominguez. Near this "Crossing of the Fathers", just a little north of Marble Canyon, another religious man, Jacob Hamblin, Mormon missionary to the Hopis, got across the river 80 years later. His crossing became the regular route for settlers traveling from Utah to Arizona. In 1872 John Lee, a fugitive accused of participating in the Mountain Meadow Massacre, established a regular ferry service in the canyon. For years the canyon was his refuge, but one day, when Lee ventured out of the gorge, he was captured and executed. Ever since, this old crossing has retained his name, Lee's Ferry.

Ferrying remained the only way a vehicle could cross the Colorado River in northern Arizona until 1929, when Navajo Bridge was constructed over Marble Canyon. It is a single arch of steel, 834 feet long, 467 feet above the river, which takes U.S. Alt. 89 across the canyon at a point where the sheer walls narrow to a width of only 600 feet. A good access road leads from the bridge down to Lee's Ferry, which is main-

LEE'S FERRY

REG

30

tained by the U.S. Park Service as a choice trout fishing area.

In 1959 a second great bridge was built a few miles up the Colorado to take U.S. 89 across Glen Canyon. It is 1271 feet long and 700 feet above the river, the highest steel arch bridge in the world. Whenever statistics lovers write about things like bridges, they love to tell how some tall structure like the Pyramids or the Leaning Tower of Pisa, could be built underneath. At Glen Canyon they've pulled a big switcheroo — they've actually built a high structure under the bridge — Glen Canyon Dam.

## TAMING "BIG RED"

**BAD COMPANY**

Glen Canyon Dam, and Hoover Dam further down the river on the Nevada border, are links in the chain of dams thrown up to imprison and rehabilitate that wild old outlaw, "Big Red" Colorado River. A description of the depredations of that turbulent waterway sounds like the script for a TV Western series — lots of violence, but a happy ending.

**WILD KID**

The Colorado (Spanish for "red") starts life high in the Rocky Mountains, just a little feller, not meanin' no harm to nobody. But soon he falls in with bad company, runnin' 'round back-alley-canyons with rough, tough mountain streams. 'Fore long he's the wildest rowdy of the lot, cuttin' up his capers through Wyoming, Colorado and Utah — always on the move. Then Big Red gets to Arizona and joins up with Li'l Colorado, as wicked a filly as ever gouged out a gorge. Together they go on a tear, ripping up the whole countryside 'round Grand Canyon. When things get too tight, they duck through Black Canyon, past Nevada and Californy, and run for the Mexican border.

**LI'L COLORADO**

From the earliest pioneer days, Big Red continues to be a holy terror, holding up travelers all along the route, ripping out bridges,

BIG RED AND LI'L

BEHIND GRAY WALLS

and behaving abominably. It's not 'til 1936 that the old public enemy is finally imprisoned behind the gray concrete walls of Hoover Dam. As other prison walls close in around him (Davis, Parker, Imperial and Glen Canyon Dams) the desperado loses his tan (from sand and silt) and becomes bluer and bluer (as sediment settles). Today he's a trusty who works in the power plant and carries water to cities and farms.

# GLEN CANYON DAM
# AND LAKE POWELL

Glen Canyon Bridge, the world's highest single steel-arch bridge, is a 1271 ft. span, 700 feet above the Colorado River. From vantage points near the bridge, especially the Visitors Center, you get grandstand views of Glen Canyon Dam. The statistics are almost as breathtaking as the view. The dam rises 580 feet above the river bed, 710 feet above the lowest point in its foundation; length of the curving crest, between the canyon walls, is 1550 feet; it is 25 feet thick at the crest, and 340 feet thick at the base, an immense wedge containing five million cubic yards of concrete.

From the Visitors Center you may take a free, self-conducted tour of the dam, in elevators that bore down through the concrete block for a closeup of the huge generators in the powerhouse.

Lake Powell backs up behind the dam for a distance of 186 miles, with numerous side canyons forming a jagged shoreline of 1860 spectacularly beautiful miles. The lake and surrounding territory is included in Glen Canyon National Recreation Area.

Page, "the town a dam built", whose first residents built the dam, lives on now that construction is finished, to serve visitors to the area. It has motels, shopping center, churches, schools — even a nine-hole golf course. Seven miles north of the dam, close to the Utah line, is Wahweap recreation center on the lake shore, with complete facilities for campers, fishermen, swimmers and water skiers. There's a dock for launching your own boat, or you may rent one. Or you may join a guided excursion cruise up the lake into a region of such breathtaking scenery that it's a shame we have to confess that most of it is in Utah, not Arizona. One of the most memorable sights you'll ever see can now be visited only a short walk from Lake Powell — it is Rainbow Bridge.

## ROCK RAINBOW

A teacup handle — that's what Rainbow Bridge looks like — a gigantic teacup handle carved of solid sandstone. It's the world's greatest natural arch, a 278 foot span, 309 feet high — you could set the nation's Capitol underneath it, with room to spare — an idea which makes them a little uneasy in Washington, D.C. It is 40 feet thick, but so beautifully shaped that it looks delicately thin. As a work of abstract sculpture this is probably Nature's greatest masterpiece. And, from its shape, it's certainly appropriate to call it Rainbow — the Navajos say it really is a rainbow, turned to stone ages ago, as the escape route used by one of their gods to get away from raging floodwaters. But, honesty compels us to report that, as a "bridge", this is never going to qualify. For one thing, Nature put it in the wrong place for a bridge — spanning a small tributary of the Colorado which nobody ever really wanted to cross. Now, if it had been built over the Colorado itself those Spaniards and Mormons might have saved a few centuries. (Though even the Mormon pioneers would have had their problems getting covered wagons over this arch.)

In 1909 Prof. Byron Cummings became the first white man to lay eyes on Rainbow Bridge, as he headed an expedition accompanied by John Wetherill, W. B. Douglass and Neill M. Judd. They penetrated the wild sandstone wilderness in search of the Rainbow, as a result of Indian tales. Noshja-Begay, Paiute Indian who had been there, guided the party. Soon after, trader Hubert Richardson laid out the old auto road across the reservation to within 14 miles of the arch. The road has been improved, but that last 14 miles is still a two-day round trip through the wildest country left in America. Rainbow Bridge National Monument is in Utah, but until Lake Powell was created, this adventurous route through Arizona was the only way to get there, unless you wanted to shoot Colorado River rapids.

Lake Powell is named for the leader of the first successful boat expedition down the Colorado and through Grand Canyon. Major John Wesley Powell, dauntless one-armed veteran of the Civil War, accomplished this feat during the summer of 1869. He started with nine men and four boats. One boat was wrecked, four men left the party, and three of these were killed by Indians. When the Major and his five survivors emerged from the labyrinth, the world learned the answer to a question it had been asking for centuries, "What is Grand Canyon really like?"

# GRAND CANYON NATIONAL PARK

The Grand Canyon is the world's No. 1 example of what can happen in the absence of "erosion control". This thousand square miles of chasm was once nothing but a little gully — a little gully that made good in a big way. If the Gov'ment had gotten down to business 50 or 100 million years earlier, "they" might have nipped it in the bud — this whole vast area might now be nice fertile farm land. But no — they pursued a "do nothing policy", and this is the result.

Grand Canyon was excavated by the Colorado River, but not by cutting downward as you might suppose. Originally it was a small stream, flowing across a level plain. Then the ground started rising — the running water, filled with sand, acted like a saw, rasping out an ever widening gash in the plain. For ages the land has continued to rise until today it has pushed up as high as 9000 feet above sea level in some places, while the Colorado, aided by all the forces of erosion, has sawed and gouged out the mighty canyon, a mile deep and as much as 18 miles from rim to rim.

This rising of the ground is nothing new. The earth's crust continuously rises and falls like the heaving bosom of an emoting movie actress. Of course, each "heave" takes a few million years, now rising mountain-high, now sinking beneath the ocean. Every time the ground is submerged a new layer of sediment is deposited. As you stand on the rim of Grand Canyon you can clearly see the different colored layers of limestone, sandstone, shale, etc., which mark successive epochs when the land was dunked in sea water.

## THE SOUTH RIM

The Grand Canyon "runs" east and west, so you will view it from the North or South Rims. The National Park is open on the South Rim all year, but the North Rim, which is more than a thousand feet higher, is closed by heavy snow during winter months.

As you walk up from the parking lot at the South Rim, there's not the slightest warning that Grand Canyon is anywhere around, 'til suddenly the world splits open at your very feet. Spread out before you is a bowl of landscape too vast for eyes to take in or mind to comprehend. You look down on whole mountain ranges — it's not uncommon to see lightning storms meandering around down there below you. It's your sense of hearing that seems to get the most definite reaction — you can "hear" the silence. The Canyon possesses the eerie

**THE CANYON IS NATURE'S FILING CABINET**

KAIBAB LIMSTONE

COCO-NINO SANDSTONE

HERMIT SHALE

TRILOBITE

CAMBRIAN AGE

1ST & 2ND ERAS

THE GROUND'S PROBABLY STILL RISING

REG

quality of blotting up sound — human chatter and other noises seem oddly muffled.

Accommodations run the gamut at the Park, from free camp grounds to swank hotels, but during summer months there never seems to be quite enough (better make advance reservations.) There are lectures and Indian dancers and free movies.

And there are the famous mule trips to the bottom of the Canyon, several miles over trails that look dangerous and are scary. But put your faith in the mule. A Grand Canyon mule is the safest means of transportation ever devised. The only "casualty" among mule passengers that we know of, was a hefty lady, roughing it for the first time in her life, who put her overalls on backward. She rode the brass buttons all the way down.

To reach Grand Canyon Village on the South Rim, turn north from U.S. 66-Int-st. 40 at Williams, 59 miles on Rte. 64. (Also from Flagstaff, 82 miles via U.S. 180.)

## LOOKING OVER THE EDGE

A paved highway, with frequent lookout points, follows the South Rim from Hermit Rest, eight miles west of the Village, to Desert View, 25 miles east. Within walking distance of Grand Canyon Village, a mile and a half by path, is Yavapai (rhymes with "have-a-pie") Point observation station, with telescopes focused on features of interest, with models, diagrams and specimens, and with a ranger-naturalist to explain it all. At this point you are about 6900 feet above sea level. The North Rim, which looks so close, is really 10 miles away as the crow flies — or 26 miles as the mule meanders. And that rim is more than 1500 feet above you, and over a mile above the river. That tiny stream you see in the Canyon depths is the Colorado, at alt. 2400 feet — and it's not so tiny. The suspension bridge used by mules to cross it is 440 feet long.

Wayside Museum, 22 miles east of the Village, has exhibits which tell the story of man in the Southwest. Nearby is Tusayan Ruin, a small partially excavated prehistoric pueblo.

The Watchtower at Desert View, three miles further east, provides one of the Canyon's most spectacular outlooks. Perched on the edge of the rim, the circular tower is built of native stone, five stories high. There's a main lobby with great windows so faultlessly clear that visiting litterbugs have tried to toss paper through the "open space" into the chasm. And when a tobacco chewer walks into the room, there's an instant alert. Beside each window is a swinging black mirror which reflects the Canyon color like the pupil of a huge eye. For a small charge you can climb the tower — on the various floors are Indian symbols, a Hopi sand painting, and on top, telescopes for long range views of the Canyon, San Francisco Peaks, colored sand country, and even the Hopi town of Moenkopi beyond Cameron.

Desert View is the eastern gateway of the National Park — and that highway you see disappearing toward Cameron is actually leading to the North Rim. Though you can seem almost to reach out and touch it in the telescope, the shortest way to the other side of the Canyon by car is via this 186-mile "end-around-run". You drive east to U.S. 89, north to the Navajo Bridge across Marble Canyon, westward on Alt. U.S. 89 past beautiful Cathedral Rock and the Vermilion Cliffs, through House Rock Valley. (If you see any bewhiskered animals, they'll not be "hippie" cattle. Arizona's state-owned buffalo herd lives in this valley.) Continue up into the Kaibab Forest, and turn south at Jacob Lake, 45 miles back to Grand Canyon again.

HOUSE ROCK

LOOK, DADDY, BEATNIK BOVINES

# THE NORTH RIM

Bright Angel Point, Point Imperial, Cape Royal and Point Sublime are North Rim vantage points which, due to their greater altitude, many consider more spectacular than those on the opposite rim. Complete accommodations, camp grounds, cabins, etc., are located at Bright Angel Point, with the lodge sitting on the very rim. The North Rim is closed by deep snow during winter months. The lodge is open from May 30 to September 30. After that date, until the road is blocked by snow, the cafeteria, cabins and camp grounds are open. And Kaibab Lodge, 18 miles north of the rim also provides accommodations during this period.

Throughout the open season nature walks, lectures, etc., are conducted by park rangers; horse trips are featured, and mule trips into the Canyon may be arranged; consult notices posted in camp and hotel. An auto caravan, accompanied by a ranger-naturalist, is conducted daily to Point Imperial and Cape Royal. It's 27½ miles each way and takes four hours.

The North Rim owes a great deal of its charm to the Kaibab Forest, a vast expanse of pine, aspen, fir, and spruce, which blankets the area adjacent to and for miles north of the Canyon. There is no section of the United States where deer may be seen in such great numbers. Most famous denison of this forest is the Kaibab White-tailed squirrel, found nowhere else in the world. As you have shrewdly guessed, its tail is snow white. You can see the squirrel and other Kaibab animals at Jacob Lake, where you turned off Alt. U.S. 89 to the Canyon.

Forty-five miles from Jacob Lake is a National Monument named after a pipe.

PLEASE! NOT WHILE I'M EATING!

# PIPE SPRING NATIONAL MONUMENT

There really is a spring at Pipe Spring, but that's not the only reason for making it a National Monument. Important as water is in Arizona, it's not that important. The principal attraction is the historic old fort, built over the spring. This was not for the purpose of protecting the water from early Californians, but to place it out of reach of marauding Indians.

The spring got its name in 1859, when William Hamblin, a member of the famous Mormon pioneer family, demonstrated his marksmanship while camping there. An old trick is to hang up a handkerchief and bet the victim he can't shoot it. The bullet will not pierce the loosely hung cloth, but will merely brush it aside. Hamblin fell for the trick. After "missing" his shot, to prove he really could shoot, Hamblin borrowed a pipe from one of the jokesters, set it on a rock near the spring, and shot the bottom out of it without grazing the inside of the bowl. Thereafter this place became known as PIPE Spring.

Eleven years later the fort was built, using local sandstone and lumber from the Kaibab Forest. Under its protection the settlers raised cattle, made butter and cheese, which was stored in the fort, kept cool by the spring water. In 1871 the first telegraph station in Arizona was established there — and the first operator was a woman, Luella Stewart. The old fort is in an excellent state of preservation, and the old spring still flows from its notch in the wall.

The National Monument is fifteen miles west of the little Mormon town of Fredonia, which is three and a half miles south of the Utah border on Alt. U.S. 89. Between the Spring and Fredonia is the finest "steamship" rock formation we've ever seen. Most so called "ship rocks" have only the vaguest resemblance to sea craft, but this one really looks like an ocean liner sailing through the desert.

# THE STRIP

At Fredonia you'll be only 50 miles from Zion National Park, one of the most beautiful spots in America. This is an Arizona book, but what-th-heck, we've got to urge you to go ahead and drive into Utah to see Zion. Besides, it's right on your way to the village of Littlefield, Arizona's first Anglo-Saxon community, settled in 1864. The only way to get there by paved roads is to drive out of Arizona and circle around through Nevada or Utah. In fact the entire section of Arizona north of the Colorado River is cut off from the rest of the state by the Grand Canyon and adjoining gorges. On the map this area, called "the Strip", looks small, but it occupies almost the same number of square miles as the whole state of New Jersey.

If you hanker to get away from the mad rush of modern living and freeway traffic, and go back in time to the days when touring could be an adventure, the Strip country should be what you're looking for. The roads are dirt and primitive — you'll need a pickup truck, or jeep, with food, water, extra gas, an axe, shovel, tire chains and camping equipment. Don't strain your eyes looking for service stations or supermarkets at every intersection. Don't strain your eyes looking for intersections.

Rough as the going is, each year several hundred people desert the pavement to drive the rugged 65 miles from Fredonia to Toroweap in Grand Canyon National Monument. Those who have seen the view of the Canyon from here say it's worth any hardship necessary to get there. At one point you can walk (or crawl) to the edge, stick your head over, and look straight down 3000 feet. A Park Service Superintendent lives at Toroweap (he has his own plane) but there are no motels or souvenir shoppes. It is definitely not a tourist trap.

# THE STRIPPERS

Back to the main highway, for those who prefer another kind of "strip" — another kind of breathtaking view of nature in the raw — 90 miles southwest of Littlefield is Las Vegas, Nevada. Here you can see the greatest entertainers, the most gorgeous girls, or if you'd rather, stand at the gaming tables and watch your money disappear. Here almost every resort hotel has its own golf course for those who want to lose athletically. From "Vegas" it's 30 miles back to Arizona 'cross the dam.

## HOOVER DAM

There's no bridge. To get from Nevada to Arizona you drive over the 1282-foot-long roadway atop Hoover Dam. Named after our 31st President, it is one of the highest dams (726 feet) in the world. If you tipped it over, it'd still be one of the highest — it is 660 feet thick at the base. They poured 4,400,000 cubic yards of concrete into the dam — enough, the tour guides will tell you, "to pave a 16-foot highway from Seattle to Miami, Florida." (Which would have been pretty narrow, even in 1936 when the dam was completed. However, by using the statistics from Glen Canyon, we could widen it to two lanes.) 96 million pounds of metal were used in Hoover Dam, and imbedded in it are more than 1000 miles of pipes, which were used to carry ice water throughout the mass of concrete. The ice water was not used to refresh thirsty workers, but to cool the structure itself. The lime in cement gets hot when mixed with water; under normal conditions it would take 150 years for the cement used in this dam to cool, so they had to use the ice water to hasten the process.

The "little" building you see huddled at the base of the dam is actually 20 stories high. It's the powerhouse where enough electricity is being generated to pay off the cost of construction, with interest, by

1987. It cost $175 million; more than $130 million has already been paid back.

# GREAT LAKES OF THE COLORADO

In the "olden days", when the muddy red Colorado River was so silt laden, folks used to say it was "too thick to drink and too thin to plow." Construction of power and irrigation dams has literally changed its color and character. From Utah to Old Mexico the water is clear and blue — and the river has expanded into a series of azure reservoirs, the Great Lakes of the Colorado. We've already described Lake Powell (page 31), 370 miles upstream from Hoover Dam, and separated from the other lakes by Grand Canyon. But Hoover Dam's Lake Mead and its satellites, Mohave and Havasu Lakes, so closely adjoin that the waters of each almost laps against the adjacent upstream dam.

LAKE MEAD, oldest of the lakes, also impounds the most water (32,471,000 acre feet when full). For more than half its 115-mile length Lake Mead is more than twice as deep as Lake Erie. It covers 229 square miles of old badlands, allowing thousands of people to go by boat into remote scenic canyons never previously seen by man. When the lake is full it's possible to sail as far as Grand Wash Cliffs at the western end of Grand Canyon. (But don't worry about the Canyon being "flooded". Even if a dam is built at Bridge Canyon it will not submerge any of the Canyon visible to National Park visitors.)

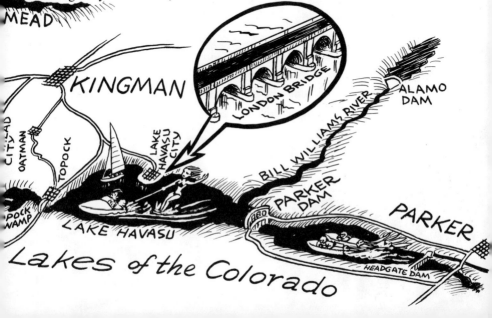

Lakes of the Colorado

Lake Mead Recreation Area, which includes the 1,699,573-acre region surrounding both Lake Mead and Lake Mohave, is administered by the Park Service just like a National Park. (A "Park" preserves natural wonders — in the "Recreation Area" lakes are man-made.) Full facilities are provided for boating, water skiing, swimming, and camping. You may bring your own boat or hire one. Lake Mead and Lake Mohave, with Havasu Lake, form a 275-mile stretch of water which is now ranked as one of the ten top fishing areas of the nation.

LAKE MOHAVE is impounded by Davis Dam, 67 miles below Hoover Dam. The northern part of the lake, fed by icy waters from the deepest part of Lake Mead, is choice trout fishing grounds. At the south end, where the lake widens and warms up, the big bass thrive.

Four resort areas are located on Lake Mohave to provide everything a fisherman could desire, from bait to launching ramps. On the Arizona side Katherine Wash serves the southern end of the lake, with Willow Beach at the northern end, 18 miles south of Hoover Dam. At Willow Beach the U.S. Fish and Wildlife Service operates a big fish hatchery for the propagation of trout. Visitors are welcome, and it is well worth the short trip from U.S. 93, whether or not you're a fishing enthusiast.

LAKE HAVASU (have-a-soo, meaning "blue water"), backed up behind Parker Dam, which is 89 miles below Davis Dam, is not included in the National Recreation Area. But Arizona and California, on opposite shores, are vying to serve fishermen and boating enthusiasts. Arizona is developing a system of parks, picnic areas, beaches and camp grounds, with good access roads. One whole new community, Lake Havasu City, has been founded on the Arizona side as a mecca for boaters. Many sport boating events are staged on the lake — Desert Regatta, in May; Boat and Ski Championships, in June; Outboard World Championships, in November.

LONDON BRIDGE? I TOLD YOU Y'WERE TAKING THE WRONG TURN!

It's at Lake Havasu City that you can see and drive across London Bridge. The bridge was dismantled in England and the 10,000 tons of granite blocks were numbered and shipped across the Atlantic to Arizona, where it was reassembled, stone by stone, in 1971.

Parker Dam is sort of like an iceberg. The 85 feet of dam that you see above river level is only the upper fourth of it. They had to sink the rest of it 235 feet below ground to set it firmly on bed rock, otherwise the river would have seeped underneath it.

The 14-mile stretch of calm water below Parker Dam, between it and Headgate Diversion Dam, near the city of Parker, has become famous as a raceway for inboard and outboard boats. So many world's records have been set for hydroplanes on this part of the Colorado that Parker has become one of the country's most important racing centers.

All highways leading to the Great Lakes of the Colorado and other irrigation reservoirs in Arizona are filled with boats of all shapes and sizes, coming and going on car-drawn trailers. We claim to have the most amphibious traffic in the world.

## COLORADO STEAMBOATS

Boating on the Colorado River began almost as soon as the U.S. took over the territory from Mexico. The military, assigned the task of enforcing open housing regulations upon local residents (Indians) who were inclined to resist integration with palefaces, chose the river as the best route then available to get supplies to their new outposts. First attempts to sail up the turbulent stream in small boats or flatboats didn't work, so a small steamboat was brought up the Gulf of California and assembled at the river's mouth. This, the first steamboat, the "Uncle Sam", arrived at old Ft. Yuma, Dec 2, 1852. Thereafter for a quarter-century, navigation of the Colorado by steamboat was continuous.

It is possible that Indian tribes in this corner of Arizona were pacified less by military force than by their own fascination at watching the steamboats. And they must have been quite a sight, clattering, belching smoke and sparks — or people, when they occasionally blew up. Of course, "peaceful" Indians could also make a pretty good thing of selling firewood to the captains.

The "Uncle Sam" ran aground and sank, within two years after launching — its successor, the "General Jesup" blew up after only seven months service. But the performance of some of the little steamers was spectacular. Late in 1857 Lt. Joseph Ives navigated his stern-wheeler, the "Explorer" all the way up the Colorado, through the deep canyon where Hoover Dam is now located, to the Virgin River.

The Mormons had hoped to use the river to supply Utah, but bucking the canyon passages proved too tough to be commercially practical. However, it became the chief thoroughfare for supplying Arizona's frontier economy until the railroads finally took over. Yuma, Ehrenberg and La Paz (once considered as a site for the territorial capital, but now a forgotten ghost town) were important river ports. In the 1870's, for $40 to $90, you could buy passage from San Francisco, by schooner around and through the Gulf, change to the riverboat below Yuma, and on up the river to one of the ports. Passengers on the stern-wheelers had staterooms, which could have doubled as sauna baths on summer days. Soldiers or "economy class" passengers could camp and sleep ashore when the boat tied up for the night. There was drinking water — in your own canteen, hung in the shade to keep "cool". A Chinese cook prepared the "complimentary" meals, served in the "salon" back of the pilot-house. Sample menu: entree — salt boiled beef; canned vegetables; fresh biscuits (sorry, no butter); dessert — peach or plum pie; coffee, black.

# KINGMAN

The first traffic along Kingman's main street was Lt. Ed Beale's camel caravan in 1857 (page 4). Only there was no street there at the time. The town wasn't founded until the railroad came through in 1883. They named the community after Lewis Kingman, who surveyed the Santa Fe line — and they named its principal thoroughfare Beale Street. Today Kingman is Arizona's gateway to Hoover Dam and the "great lakes": southwest 50 miles to the Colorado River bridge at Topock, and 59 miles to Lake Havasu City; due west 33 miles to Davis Dam; and northwest 72 miles to Hoover Dam.

Twenty miles north of Kingman, and four miles east of U.S. 93, you can see a remarkable "yesterday and today" contrast in mining. In 1870 the twin boomtowns of Chloride and Mineral Park came into existence, serving hundreds of newly discovered silver mines in the region. Miners were being paid $5 per day (no deductions) and were paying $1 a can for canned food, and $1 a pound for coffee and sugar. Two thousand mines had been recorded in the area by 1876 and a number of silver and gold mills were in operation. Sheet metal for the mills came from England, by way of steamboats up the Colorado, and millions of dollars in silver were sent back down the river to the world's money marts. Mineral Park listed its population as 400 (with four saloons), while Chloride hit a peak population of 2000 in 1900.

Then the silver mines closed and most of the mining camps quietly perished. Chloride, however, never completely died, and citizens who stayed on were not happy to have it called a "ghost town". You can still see the abandoned mines and mills 'round there — but if there were ever any ghosts they have been rudely evicted in the last few years. Right next door in Mineral Park they've opened one of Arizona's newest, most modern "open pit" copper mines — a development made

LT. BEALE

LEW KINGMAN

possible by profitable techniques of "steam shovel" excavation of low grade ore. And now they have another mill to replace the little old ones, the world's largest grinding mill with the latest in radioactive measuring devices and electronic loading equipment.

Further north you can visit the ghost town of White Hills, a favorite of photographers, with its abandoned little frame stores, its row of wooden houses and pitiful graveyard. It is only 5½ miles from U.S. 93, 44 miles from Kingman to the turnoff. Thirty miles west of Kingman via the paved highway which used to be U.S. 66 is the old gold camp of Oatman, definitely no ghost city, but enjoyed by photogs for its board walks and old buildings.

## THE JOSHUA TREES

Kingman lies midway between two great forests of plants which look like something left over from the Paleozoic ages. They are the Joshua trees, some growing 35 feet high, with fistfulls of green pointed dagger-leaves, held high by twisting arms. The arms are covered by a mat of light brown "hair" — dead leaves of past growth. The Joshua in bloom is a real show, with flowering stalks clutched above each leafy fist, sometimes dozens to the plant. If the flower clusters look like lilies to you, don't be surprised, for that's exactly what they are. The Joshua is the largest of the desert Yucca plants, that family of lilies which Nature has adapted to life in arid climes. (See page 71).

One of the Joshua forests may be seen along the Pierce Ferry road, which branches off of U.S. 93, 32 miles north of Kingman. The forest extends for 30 miles along the road, to within seven miles of Lake Mead. Not even Joshua Tree National Monument in California can boast finer specimens than grow here.

Between Kingman and Wickenburg is the Arizona Joshua Forest Parkway, which extends for 17 miles along both sides of U.S. 93 — a desert area where thousands of the strange trees are preserved in their natural state.

## THE MOGOLLON RIM

Sometime back in the Mesozoic age, Arizona almost broke in two. It was during one of the periodic upheavals of the earth's crust, and the northeastern quarter of the state lifted up, right according to the geological script, but land to the south missed its cue and failed to rise. The resulting split in the landscape must have left local residents, dinosaurs and flying reptiles, considerably shook-up. Today the dinosaurs are gone, but you can still plainly see where the big crack-up occurred. On the maps it is identified as the Mogollon (muggy-yone) Rim — in Zane Grey's famous novels it's called the "Tonto Rim".

The Rim is a 200-mile-long wall of cliffs, like a rugged coast line, which at places rises a thousand feet above the ocean of pines. Actually there are pines above and below the Rim — it cuts through unbroken forest throughout its entire length. All north-south roads in the eastern half of Arizona provide breathtaking views as they scramble down the Rim, notably the zig-zag drop into Oak Creek Canyon, the awesome but superbly engineered descent at Strawberry Hill, and the Coronado Trail, spectacular plunge from the forest altitudes to desert lowlands, near the New Mexico line. A forest road, open except during severe winter weather, winds along the Rim, starting near Verde Hot Springs on the west, and connecting with Rte. 288 between Young and Heber.

When fully developed and paved, this will be known as Zane Grey Highway, one of the state's finest scenic drives, extending all the way to Pinetop.

## ARIZONA'S BIG TIMBER

For those who have always thought of Arizona only in terms of deserts and cacti, it may come as something of a shock to learn that one fourth of the entire state is covered by forest growth — not Joshua trees, not petrified trees, but honest to goodness wood trees. From the Grand Canyon, one vast stand of timber spreads southward in a 300-mile semi-circle into New Mexico. In places this piny blanket is 60 miles wide. It is the largest unbroken Ponderosa pine forest in America. (Its spine is the Mogollon Rim.)

Not all of Arizona's forests are in the northern part of the state. Wherever you find high mountains, you'll find them topped by the big trees. There are lofty ranges in southern Arizona with forest-clad slopes that extend clear to the Mexican border. Some large stands of trees are on Indian reservations, and on state and private lands, but most of the timber is located in seven National Forests. Lumbermen estimate that the Ponderosa pine in these National Forests contain 13 billion board feet of lumber, with another billion-plus in Douglas fir.

With all this timber, you'd think lumbering would be an important industry in Arizona, and in fact it is. In early territorial days sawmills turned out timbers for mines and bridges, and ties for railroads. One sawmill near Payson has operated continuously since 1879. But the only streams in Southwest forests are trout creeks, too small to float logs, so Arizona lumbering had to wait for development of motor transport to come into its own. Today, besides a lot of small sawmills, there are several really large ones. At the two largest, in

Flagstaff and McNary, visitors are welcome to follow the big logs from millpond to debarker, to huge circular saws where they're cut into various lengths, and on to be sliced into boards by the 50-foot band saws.

At McNary the Southwest Forest Industries' moulding factory is the largest in the world, capable of making 3000 different patterns for inside and outside trimming.

## THE PAPER MILL

Arizona's greatest lumber operation is the Southwest Forest Industries' $32 million Pulp and Paper Mill, which produces newsprint, 75,000 tons per year (that's a lot of newspapers), and 65,000 tons per year of kraft and linerboard (that's a lot of wrapping paper). The mill, 15 miles west of Snowflake, is the only pulp and paper plant in the world not built on a river or tidewater. It takes great quantities of trees and water to run a paper mill — but at this site you see only a few scrub oak and juniper, and definitely no river. Well, the wood is trucked in, logs from the mountains, and waste lumber from the sawmills. And the water, eight million gallons a day, is pumped 750 feet from an underground "lake" of saturated sandstone, 60 miles wide, 140 miles long, and 400 feet thick. Chemical-laden waste is floated away from the mill, eight and a half miles to an old dry lake, where it can't pollute Arizona streams.

By the way, are you interested in place names? Snowflake was named after its founders, two Mormon bishops, Erastus Snow and William Flake.

## FISH IN THE PINES

It's true there are no rivers in Arizona's great pine forest suitable for floating logs to market, but that's not to imply there are no streams at all. There are, in fact, many creeks, originating in springs above and below the Mogollon Rim. They flow north and south, eventually join-

ing up to form the source of all the state's principal rivers. And by the grace of the State Game and Fish Dept., the National Forest Service, and the Apache Indians, they are also the source of enormous pleasure for trout fishermen. Each year anglers spend $40 million or more in Arizona in pursuit of fish and happiness, much of it in the Rim country. That's a sizeable investment, so it seems only fair to make sure they have happiness, and plenty of fish, to pursue. Without considerable help, the fish would never be able to keep up with the demand. The help is provided by three state operated trout hatcheries — Sterling Springs in Oak Creek Canyon, Page Springs near Cottonwood, and Tonto Creek underneath the Rim, north of Kohl's Ranch resort. (There are also two U.S. Fish and Wildlife trout hatcheries on the Fort Apache Reservation.) Rainbow, brook, and brown trout by the millions are hatched and reared each year. Fingerling-sized trout are planted in small lakes and reservoirs, where they grow rapidly in the quiet waters. In the many creeks where currents are boisterous, and the fishermen are numerous, fish are not planted until they are "catchable" size, ready for the fight.

The principal trout fishing areas in the Rim country, reading from west to east are: around Flagstaff, long-time popular lakes; Oak Creek Canyon; around Payson, below the Rim, the Tonto and other fabulous creeks; above the Rim, along the Zane Grey Highway, the state has dammed a number of streams, creating a network of small, well stocked lakes; the Fort Apache Reservation, numerous fine streams and lakes; and the Greer-Springerville-White Mountain area with lakes, rushing creeks and happy fishermen.

Around the lakes and along the streams, the Forest Service provides many and varied facilities for sportsmen. Some are very complete, with stores, campgrounds, trailer spaces, water, fireplaces, toilets, etc. others have minimum conveniences, and may even require a short

hike to reach them. On the reservation, Indians welcome fishermen and provide excellent facilities of all kinds.

Fishing isn't the only sport in Arizona's pine lands — the forest is populated with all kinds of big game which attract hunters in season. Number one, of course, is the deer, but there are also antelope, wild turkey, occasional black bear and several kinds of predatory animals. In case you had the idea that this country has gone tame, the last report we saw listed bounties paid on more than 100 mountain lions killed one winter in Arizona.

If you should hear moaning, groaning, or shrieks of downright anguish resounding 'mongst the pines, don't panic. Chances are it will not be the victim of an attacking lion — but only the pitiful cry of a happily suffering golfer. Golf has come to the forest with the increasing droves of summer residents, attracted by cool altitudes. They have settled on the outskirts of established towns or, where private land or government leases were available, have created whole new communities. Now most settlements, old or new, have their golf courses. Several are among the state's most beautiful and testing eighteens.

## OAK CREEK CANYON AND SEDONA

South of Flagstaff the super "Black Canyon" route to Phoenix, which will become Interstate 17, is fast and beautiful, but it by-passes Oak Creek Canyon. We urge, therefore, that you leave it and take the narrower, but paved canyon route, via Alt. U.S. 89. A few miles from "Flag" you reach the lookout point on the rim, where you can stand and see cars zig-zag all the way down to Oak Creek past the fish hatchery. From there the road follows the rapidly dropping creek, heavily stocked with trout, and lined with camp grounds, cabins and resorts among the pines. In the summer it may be hard to find even a parking space without advance reservations, it's that popular. When you break out of the pines at Sedona, turn and look back at Oak

Creek Canyon's brilliant red and yellow ochre walls, rising in "sculptured" cathedral shapes above the trees. Many painters have settled around Sedona, but they face a frustrating future here. To try to paint this scene is enough to drive an artist mad — it is already too colorful to be exaggerated, and any attempt to "copy Nature" would seem too imaginative and overdone. Motor hotels and eating places are arranged to have large windows for viewing the scene, the most stu-pen-juss picture window views you may ever gaze upon.

This has long been a favorite spot for Hollywood picture makers, so you may recognize the canyon backdrops for scores of movie Westerns.

South of here the canyon opens out into the broad Verde Valley. From the other side of the valley, as you look back at the colored cliffs, you get the feeling of being back in Painted Desert country again.

## VERDE VALLEY

In the late 1200s, when prehistoric people were abandoning Wupatki and other pueblos north of Flagstaff, there was a population boom in Verde Valley, as refugees from the drouth moved in. To folks from water starved lands, the Valley's irrigation agriculture was most attractive. Montezuma Castle and Tuzigoot National Monument preserve superb examples of cliff dwellings built to take care of the population explosion. Then, suddenly, these people, too, walked out on all their homes — but nobody has figured out why they left or where they went. When Spanish soldiers, under command of Antonio de Espejo, came into Verde Valley in 1583, the old habitations were in ruins.

In 1864 pioneer settlers along the Verde River comprised a minority group, discriminated against by local residents, the Apaches. Volunteers from Whipple Barracks, near Prescott, came in and set up Camp Lincoln to protect them. Twenty years later it became Fort

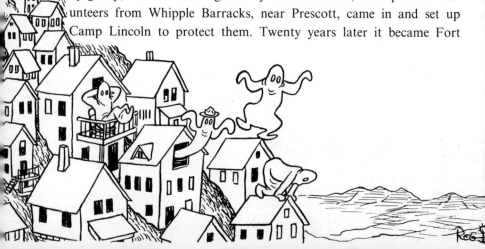

Verde, under command of regular troops. Today at Camp Verde, you can see pioneer relics in the Fort Verde Museum, housed in the original building which garrisoned the U.S. Cavalry.

At the northern end of the valley are, Cottonwood, and the old copper smelting town of Clarkdale. High above on the mountainside is the famous old town of Jerome, beside the now dug-out copper mines. Jerome was once one of Arizona's largest cities, perched so precariously on the mountain that a man could step from his back porch right into his neighbor's chimney. Many of the old houses are still hanging there, but most of the people are gone. However, the Jerome Historical Society maintains a Mine Museum there, and the "living ghost town" remains a very popular tourist attraction.

## TUZIGOOT

When you realize that Phoenix, the capital city of Arizona, is less than 90 years old, it becomes impressive to learn that Tuzigoot was one of Arizona's principal towns for more than three centuries. Tuzigoot National Monument, near Clarkdale, preserves the excavated ruins of the pueblo which flourished between 1100 and 1450 A.D. Located on a limestone ridge, 120 feet above the Verde River, it covers the summit, and is terraced part way down the slopes. There are 110 quite large rooms, averaging 12 by 18 feet, arranged in typical pueblo style, in places two stories high. The pueblo is 500 feet long and as much as 100 feet across. The people entered their rooms by climbing ladders to the rooftops, and from there through hatchways in the ceilings.

The first hundred years are the toughest, they say — actually Tuzigoot did not grow much for the first two centuries, remaining a village of 15 or 20 rooms, with the population seldom going over 50. Then came the refugees from the big drouth at Wupatki, and within 25

years Tuzigoot doubled and redoubled in size, till it could boast a population of 200 or 300 living within the "city limits", and farming along the river below. The "metropolitan population" was far greater, for within sight of Tuzigoot, half a dozen other large pueblos came into being. The community continued to thrive for another hundred years before enemy invaders, or pestilence, or some other force caused all the towns to be abandoned.

The ruins were excavated by University of Arizona archaeologists in 1933-34 and, since no amateurs had dug into it before, its rich treasure of artifacts, painted pottery, rare turquoise mozaics, as well as skeletal remains of some former citizens, are preserved complete in the Monument museum.

One discovery at Tuzigoot suggests (to us at least) that these people must have figured two heads are better than one. In one room of the ruin an archaeologist reported he found a "total of eight skulls, and bones of only four skeletons." No further explanation.

## MONTEZUMA CASTLE AND WELL

The unknown pioneer who named Montezuma Castle should have done real well in Hollywood, titling movies. Everything about the name is wrong. It's not a "castle", but a large apartment house, built high up in a cliff cave. And Montezuma, the great Aztec emperor of ancient Mexico, never even heard of the place.

The cliff dwelling was built during the population boom around 1300 A.D., about the time Tuzigoot was experiencing its greatest growth a few miles away. The building is four stories high, with two rooms below the first floor serving as a basement. Since these rooms are 80 feet above the valley floor, this makes it one of the country's

highest basements. The walls of the Castle apartments are about a foot thick, formed of rough chunks of limestone held together with clay mortar. Roof timbers are logs, the largest of which are ten feet long and a foot in diameter. These logs were cut with stone axes, and hauled up the cliff by hand, without pulleys, using home made ropes. The whole thing was built without any kind of metal tools. . .nor any kind of gov'ment financing. Ceilings were made by laying poles crossways on the log beams, overlaying these with willows or coarse grass. It was finished off with a three or four inch layer of mud, which became the floor of the apartment above.

About 50 people, 12 or 15 families, lived in the 20 rooms of Montezuma Castle. This may seem a little crowded, but life in a cliff dwelling had its advantages. The view was terrific, and you were not troubled by bill collectors. They had guards stationed in two little cubbyholes at the bottom of the cliff to keep uninvited guests off the ladders. There were no light bills nor taxes. And water was free — if you wanted water, the little woman simply scrambled down 80 feet of ladders, scooped up a large jugful from the creek below, and clambered back up again. (The men had a sort of "union" which frowned upon males wasting time at such feminine tasks as carrying water.)

Fire was somewhat of a problem in cliff apartments. It was common practice to build your fire in the middle of the room, on the floor. This was O.K. as long as the mud didn't wear too thin, and let the fire get into the willows underneath. With all the smoke in the room, this could be hard to detect until you dropped in on the family in the flat below.

Montezuma Castle National Monument is one of the most convenient cliff dwellings for the visitor, only a short drive from the main

highway, and a very short walk from the parking lot. There is an excellent visitors' center.

Seven miles by road, northeast of the Castle, but part of the National Monument, is Montezuma Well (which also has no relationship to the Aztec ruler). The Well looks like someone had scooped out a great cup-shaped hole, and half filled it with water. Actually it is a limestone sink, where the roof of a large underground cave fell in. The lake in the bottom is 70 feet below the rim, 400 feet across and 55 feet deep. It is fed by springs which have a constant flow of a million and a half gallons every day. The water bores an exit under the rim into nearby Beaver Creek, which flows past Montezuma Castle. Ruins of two large pueblos are located near the Well, and some small cave dwellings are seen in the rim itself. Prehistoric inhabitants used waters of the Well for irrigation. You can still see their ditches, "fossilized" by water so heavily mineral-laden that it coated the canals with lime "cement". Southeast of Verde Valley, on another tributary of the Verde River below Mogollon Rim, is Tonto Natural Bridge, made entirely from lime deposits of mineral springs.

## TONTO NATURAL BRIDGE

Below the Mogollon Rim, not far from Strawberry Hill, between Pine and Payson, a rough little side road leads to Tonto Natural Bridge. As we have previously noted, Nature is a marvelous bridge builder, with no respect whatsoever for highway engineering. Tonto Bridge is a perfect example. Here is a great arch, 183 feet high, 400 feet long, wide enough and substantial enough to accommodate a fleet of buses traveling abreast. It is the world's largest "travertine" arch, laboriously built with minute layers of limestone "plaster", deposited a drop at a time by mineral springs. Of course, it took ages to complete. But did Nature place it over some river on a road where it would do some good? She did not! She put it across tiny Pine Creek,

three miles from the main highway. You can drive to it, and on it —
but that's as far as you can go, for Nature, in one last defiant gesture,
jammed Tonto Bridge against the side of a mountain.

The Bridge is privately owned. Accommodations are provided in
an atmosphere of hospitality reminiscent of "grampa's ol' farm", with
home cooking, served ranch style. There's a farm right on top of the
Bridge. A short walk, over good foot paths, takes you down the canyon to a vantage point from which you can see the arch. Underneath
you will see the constant "rainfall" from dripping springs which are
still at work depositing calcium to enlarge the structure. Paths also
lead to small crystal caves and to a little waterfall, where articles left
in the spray collect a limestone coating and "turn to rock".

## UNPLEASANTNESS IN PLEASANT VALLEY

Another famous spot below the Rim, in "Zane Grey country",
is Pleasant Valley, which has always looked as peaceful as it does
today. Yet there was a time, in the 1880s, when any man who rode
into the valley would have been an extremely poor insurance risk.
Pleasant Valley has a most unpleasant history.

The Graham-Tewkesbury feud is commonly referred to as a cattle-
sheep war, but it started as a quarrel between rival cow camps. One
outfit claimed it had first right to all the range land in the valley. The
other disputed that claim, and words were backed by bullets. One of
the outfits brought a herd of sheep to the valley, adding insult to
injury. Ranch houses became forts. Men were killed from ambush.
No man ventured to ride the range alone if he valued his neck. Before it ended, 37 were dead and survivors had been reduced almost to
the vanishing point.

Zane Grey's classic novel, "To The Last Man", was inspired by
this old feud, as were other Westerns, but every fictionalized account
has always brought bitter reaction from survivors or their kin. "The
last man" to die violently in the feud, Tom Graham, was actually shot

in Tempe, Arizona, after leaving Pleasant Valley. One of the Tewkesburys was tried for the murder, but was not convicted.

Today in Young, a most pleasant little town in the center of Pleasant Valley, residents will point out an old house, here and there, and call attention to the sinister little loopholes — "just right for shootin' outta" — and occasionally you may find someone who "will talk" about the feud, but the stories are vague, and seldom check with others you may have heard.

## CANYON OF THE SALT

You've been told that descents from Mogollon Rim are breathtaking, but U.S. 60 heading southwest from Show Low, doesn't live up to that billing. It goes down in long, gradual sweeps through pleasant but unexciting landscape. As the miles pass there's nothing to indicate that this will turn into one of the most memorable drives you may ever experience. U.S. 60 slopes across the Apache reservation, past the Carrizo junction with Rte. 73 to Fort Apache. No danger from the Indians, though, unless you happen to run into one of their pickup trucks and wreck your car.

Twenty-five miles further down the road, you come upon signs reading, "Steep Grades" or "Trucks Check Brakes" — and then you swing around a curve and arrive at the first viewpoint overlooking Salt River Canyon. There are several excellent lookouts on either side of this gorge. 'Way down at the bottom is a toy bridge crossing a miniature rivulet — tiny cars are plainly visible creeping along the ribbon which winds up the cliffs across the way. Driving down into the canyon, you happily discover the "ribbon" is a wide, wonderfully engineered highway which retains the thrill without the hazard. The bridge turns out to be a full sized span across the life sized Salt River.

TOY BRIDGE
AND TINY CARS

Near the bridge are service station, restaurant, etc., and below, along the river is a rest and picnic area. Views from either side of the canyon are equally beautiful, and soaring out of the depths on that superb road is almost as impressive as the descent. U.S. 60 continues 45 miles to Globe.

The Salt River is the boundary which separates Arizona's two Apache reservations, Ft. Apache on the north, and San Carlos to the south. State Rte. 73 winds through Ft. Apache Reservation from its eastern border, through McNary, White River, Ft. Apache, and on to the junction with U.S. 60. U.S. 70 crosses San Carlos Reservation east of Globe.

## APACHE LAND

In pioneer days the very mention of Apache Indians was enough to make a man's scalp tingle, and not without good reason. The Spaniards, Mexicans, and American settlers, each in their turn had found that personal contact with Apaches all too often resulted in acute and premature baldness. Led by chieftains like Cochise and Geronimo, Apaches made life hectic and uncertain in Arizona, even for neighboring Indian tribes. So frightful was their reputation, that even now travelers feel a little skittish about visiting Apache country. If you have such thoughts, put your mind at ease. Visitors are not only safe, they are welcomed on the reservations.

In fact, on the Fort Apache Reservation, tribesmen make it their business to welcome visitors — big business! At last count they had erected dams creating 33 excellent trout lakes. The 300 miles of rushing mountain brooks in the Apache-White Mountains area have always rated high with trout fishermen. Two government fish hatcheries keep reservation waters well stocked. The tribe is busily developing modern motor courts, service stations, stores, camp sites and other facilities along highways and near lakes.

San Carlos Reservation has become famous for cattle raising. TV fans who have learned about Indians and cowboys from the Westerns are going to be pretty mixed up when they find out that on the Apache Reservation the cowboys ARE the Indians. And the most confused fans of all have got to be the children of Apache cowboys. In this electronic age, many of the Indians have television, and like all kids, their favorite programs are the Westerns.

San Carlos herds of pure bred cattle are among the best in the world. Tribal cattle associations manage the herds, and even maintain one "social security herd" for care of needy aged Apaches.

## NAKED TRUTH ABOUT SAVAGES

In some respects Indians and Whites have switched places since pioneer days. In the matter of clothing, for instance, the White settlers' womenfolk, modestly clad in petticoats and mother hubbards, were shocked by the scanty attire of native residents of Arizona. No effort was spared to reform the "nekkid savages". The campaign was an outstanding success. To this day it is not unusual to see Apache women wearing voluminous dresses which would have been completely modest in nineteenth century feminine styles. But what of the great grandchildren of those "shocked" pioneer ladies? They are the lasses you see in supermarkets, clad in little more than halter and gee-string. Today it's not the naked savages who are naked. Nor savage, for that matter.

In spite of the coming of the auto, electricity, and other items of White Man's culture, the Apache has not completely cut all ties with the ways and beliefs of his fathers. It may be a little disappointing to find so many Indians living in ordinary rectangular houses, but you'll

YESTERDAY          TODAY

still see plenty of traditional wickiups throughout the reservations. The wickiup, like the Navajo hogan, is a single-room dwelling, built in the shape of a small dome. It is constructed by setting poles in a circle, then bowing them inward to form the dome-shaped framework. This is plastered with layers of mud and bear grass, overlaid with assorted pieces of hide, canvas, tin, as available. Like the hogan, a wickiup's door always opens to the east.

Artistically, the Apaches' principal claim to fame is basketry. Huge Apache storage and burden baskets are unexcelled in craftsmanship and design. The women are also skilled beadworkers. Genuine items of Apache handcraft may be purchased at the Arts and Crafts store in the town of Bylas, on U.S. 70, where it crosses San Carlos Reservation and at other trading posts on both Apache reservations.

# FATHER OF THE GIRL

These days in U.S. cultural centers, only the wealthiest of papas can afford the debut of a marriageable daughter in one of those high society "coming out" parties. For an Apache father the financial crisis is almost as great in the reservation social whirl. As in the White Man's world, it is a sort of status thing, and a well fixed dad can find himself stuck with a party costing a sizeable chunk of his wealth. Friends and relatives come from far and near to partake of the free food for three days, all at dear ol' dad's expense, and to gambol and gamble, and generally have a high time. Sometimes several fathers combine to share the cost of feeding the multitudes, hiring dancers, and staging a really big ceremonial for their daughters.

A coming out ceremony is a physical ordeal for the girls, who wear elaborate costumes of buckskin (rented by dad, of course) fringed

with tiny bells, which tinkle through the days and nights of almost continuous dancing. During rest periods for the girls, assembled guests join in "social dances" around the huge bonfire, to the slow rhythm of an "all-drum orchestra", beating time on dried cowhides. High point of the affair is the appearance of the famous Apache "devil dancers", wearing black masks and large headpieces, which look like impressionist art creations. They come to chase away the evil spirits.

The grand finale comes as the rising sun touches the heads of the kneeling girls. An attendant brushes their hair with a thin golden paste, made of meal and pollen, for fertility. Any left over pollen potion is dabbed on the heads of babes, held out by their anxious mothers, or splashed with generous abandon over those crowding around, thus spreading fertility willy-nilly among the spectators.

## CORONADO TRAIL

As Flagstaff has its San Francisco Peaks overlooking one end of the Mogollon Rim, so Springerville has its Mt. Baldy looking down from its lofty 11,590 foot altitude on the Rim's other end. Old Baldy and its sister peak, Mt. Ord, dominate the White Mountains. Water originating in their winter snow packs ends up as drinking water in Los Angeles, and helps irrigate rich farm land around Phoenix.

South of Springerville, U.S. 666, alias the Coronado Trail, passes in the shadow of Mt. Baldy, through magnificent stands of pine, spruce, and quaking aspen, to Hannagan Meadow and, just beyond, the Rim. Looking south from this 9000 foot elevation is like a view from an astronaut's window, into the distant blue haze which is old Mexico, whence Coronado came in 1540 A.D. The trail descends spectacularly to Clifton, more than a mile nearer sea level, winding past Blue Range Primitive Area, the largest remaining wilderness in Arizona — remote country, accessible only by foot or horseback.

The Springerville-Clifton scenic highway is named after Francisco Vasquez de Coronado, the famous Spaniard who took a trip through this part of Arizona three centuries before the forty-niners crossed the state in covered wagons. Coronado evidently had a great interest in road construction, because he traveled all the way from Mexico just to investigate a street paving project. He had heard that "the Seven Cities of Cibola" had streets paved with gold. Actually the "Cities of Cibola" were the Zuni villages — they're still there, 55 miles from St. Johns, just across the Arizona state line in New Mexico. And then, as now, the only gold in the streets of these villages was the reflected light of the sunset. Coronado scouted as far east as Kansas, and he sent some of his men to look at the Hopi villages, but nowhere did they find any 24 carat streets. So Coronado went back down the trail to Mexico, bitterly disappointed that he had nothing concrete to show for his research in golden road building.

## EARLY TRAIL TRAVELERS

Many historians contend that Coronado didn't travel the route 'twixt Clifton and Springerville which bears his name, but more likely passed through the Ft. Apache region. However, in Arizona's territorial days, there is no doubt whatever that some of the West's wildest characters did come this way. There was Ike Clanton, for instance, who had a disagreement with a certain Marshal Wyatt Earp, of Tombstone. He found the air pollution (atmosphere filled with lead) in the tough frontier town a threat to his health, so departed hurriedly for the more salubrious climate of the White Mountains. There, with other "health seekers", he laid plans to go into the new railroad business (robbing the trains). They needed dynamite for blowing up Santa Fe rails, but the proprietor of Springerville's general store, Gus Becker, refused to sell. And when big Ike tried to force the issue, frightening the store's customers, Gus, a rather small man, knocked the outlaw flat. Then he

BECKER'S STORE

dragged Ike to the door, and heaved him into the street, at the feet of his astonished "associates", waiting around outside.

Not long after, Ike received an even harsher indication that he was not appreciated in the neighborhood. A posse of local ranchers "shot him daid".

At the lower end of the Coronado Trail, a decade earlier, another posse, chasing another band of outlaws, played its part in starting one of the world's most fabulous mining developments. Bob and Jim Metcalf, a pair of brothers riding with the sheriff, spied an outcropping of ore in the steep canyon along the San Francisco River, and came back later to stake out claims. The ore turned out to be rich in copper. The millions which have been taken out of that canyon in the years since, would have made Coronado's wildest dreams seem hardly worth a yawn.

Metcalf, Morenci and Clifton sprang into life as roaring mining camps. Apaches made life unpredictable for freighters hauling ore the eight miles from Metcalf to the smelter in Clifton, so Arizona's first railway was built. The first locomotive, "Little Emma", was hauled 600 miles by oxen, from Colorado. It may be seen today at Arizona Museum in Phoenix.

The town of Metcalf is no longer there, but Clifton and Morenci are very much alive. At Morenci is the nation's second largest open pit mine. In modern Clifton you can still see traces of the old pioneer town — the original jail f'rinstance. It was small, but prisoners stayed put. The jail was blasted out of solid rock in the cliff side. The man who built it was so proud of his job, that he celebrated its completion too enthusiastically. He became the first guest.

# WHERE COPPER COMES FROM

Today Arizona produces more copper than all the other 49 states combined. And the oldest copper mining area in the state at the foot

LITTLE EMMA

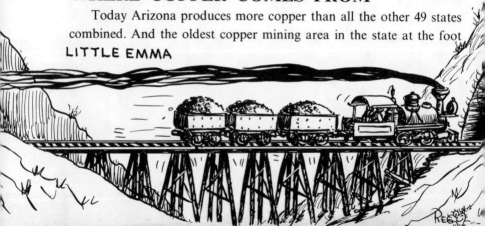

of the Coronado Trail is still one of the greatest. The Morenci mine produces more than $60 million worth of the red metal every year.

Flying over Arizona you may get the idea that they're building stadiums all over the state, carved out of stone, with rows of seats in tiers of steps around the great ovals. If your plane gets low enough, you may see toy trains and/or trucks moving along the tiers. These "stadiums" are actually open pit copper mines, the "toys" are gigantic vehicles, and the "benches" are 50 feet high.

In the old days, pioneer copper miners got out the ore by drilling holes for the blasting powder, using sledge hammers, drills, and their own muscle power. It was an art at which proud hard rock experts used to compete on festive occasions. Of course, ore dug out by hand had to be very rich "high grade" material, to make mining profitable. Modern, electrically operated drills, earth moving machinery, and up-to-date ways of recovering even small amounts of metal from "low grade" ore have made the open pit mine practical and economically feasible.

In an underground mine, you tunnel into the mountain to get to the copper — in an open pit mine you simply dig up the whole mountain. Before producing any copper at all in this type of mine, you have to scrape away the top layer of just plain rock. This "waste" will be perhaps 200 feet deep. At Morenci, for instance, they had to haul away 50 million tons of this "capping" before they could even begin to scoop out copper ore.

Of course Arizona still has its underground mines, like the great diggings at Superior, San Manuel, three big mines at Bisbee, and numerous small mines. But the open pit operations are the largest and most spectacular. Most of them have observation stations and tours. Besides the famed Morenci mine, you may see open pits at Ajo (New Cornelia), the Globe-Miami district (Inspiration, Copper Cities, Blue

Bird, Ox Hide), southwest of Tucson (Twin Buttes, Pima, Esperanza, Mission), northwest of Tucson (Silver Bell), west of Prescott (Bagdad), Ray (Mineral Creek) and Kingman (Mineral Park). At Bisbee you can see where the mountain called "Sacramento Hill" used to stand — it is now known as "Sacramento Pit", and is now worked out. But another open pit operation is going full tilt near Bisbee, at the huge Lavender Pit.

## ARIZONA DESERT

On any of the roads which drop off the Mogollon Rim, you descend a mile or so of altitude, through changing vegetation, till you get into the Southwest desert. If your idea of desert is a Sahara wasteland of sand, with sparse tufts of buffalo grass hanging on for dear life between the dunes, you'll have to revise your mental picture when you see the "desert" that blankets Southern Arizona. A study of the Weather Department's records makes it hard to believe that anything could live on such a stingy ration of rainfall. But Nature has developed a surprising variety of plants which not only can survive on almost no water, but grow and put out exotic blossoms and delicious fruit. These plants are so constructed that they can quickly soak up excess water during rare rainy spells, and store it for months or years.

Contrary to popular belief, everything on the desert which has stickers is not a "cactus". Botanically, a cactus is closely related to the common rose, and the blossoms are every bit as beautiful as anything your florist can produce. Other plant families, like the lily, are well represented in the desert, and we'll identify some of them for you a little later. Among the cacti, unquestionably the monarch of America's desert, is that giant native of Arizona, the saguaro.

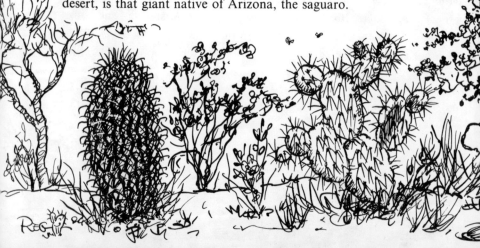

# THE GIANT OF ARIZONA

The *saguaro* (sah-WAH-ro), also known as the Giant Cactus, is Number One among all desert plants of the Southwest, first in size, first in longevity, and first by vote of the Arizona legislature, which designated its blossom the State Flower. The saguaro has a single trunk, straight and thick as a telephone pole, and often as tall. Branches grow from this trunk, sometimes by the score. The branchless ones, a mere ten or twelve feet high, are youngsters, probably not more than 50 years old. You can judge the age of a Giant Cactus with fair accuracy, by its height. On the average it will grow about two inches a year. Arms may grow with perfect symmetry, like a candelabra, or comically twisted like a man trying to reach the itchy spot on his back.

The saguaro trunk and branches are corregated, top to bottom, which allows the plant to expand a la accordion, to store more water in its pulpy interior during rainy weather. In this way it can retain enough moisture to last as long as four years without a refill. Look closely and you'll see that every ridge is studded with warts, set close together. Each wart is a tiny pincushion filled with big "darning needles" sticking out at all angles.

To complete your examination of the saguaro, hunt around the desert until you find a dead one lying on the ground. Note the skeletal framework of woody rods, one for each accordion ridge. When erect, these rods support the Giant's tons of weight, with flexible strength, "engineered" by Nature to allow the huge plant to sway in strong desert winds, without breaking. Roots spread out from the plant in a large circular network, only inches below the surface of the ground, forming a plumbing system to gather in moisture over a wide area, and rapidly pipe it to the plant for storage.

In April or May the saguaro blooms, the tip of every branch holding aloft bouquets of waxy white flowers, a new bouquet each morning, since each blossom lasts only about 12 hours. The saguaro is a nocturnal bloomer — its flowers open about midnight, and close by noon next day. Each blossom gives way to edible fruit, with lots of tiny black seeds, which ripens in midsummer. When ripe, the fruit splits open, exposing the brilliant crimson inside, which is often mistaken for a red flower. For centuries the Indians have harvested saguaro fruit, using long poles made from saguaro ribs. The fruit could be eaten fresh, made into preserves, or dried like figs. They also pound the shiny seeds into flour.

Near Tucson, at the Saguaro National Monument, splendid stands of the Giants may be seen in their natural state, with many other native desert plants. In many parts of central and southern Arizona you will see mountainsides covered with forests of the Giants. Except for a very few specimens which have straggled over its borders, the saguaro is an Arizona monopoly. If you see a movie with saguaros in the background, it's almost a certainty that it was filmed in this state.

## THE ORGAN PIPE

The *Pitahaya* (pea-TAH-yuh) organ pipe cactus is closely related to the saguaro, and a single "pipe" might easily be mistaken for a branch of the Giant. But it is not difficult to tell the difference between the full grown plants. Where the saguaro is a "tree", with branches curving out of a massive trunk, the organ pipe is a large "bush", branching at the ground, without a predominating central "trunk".

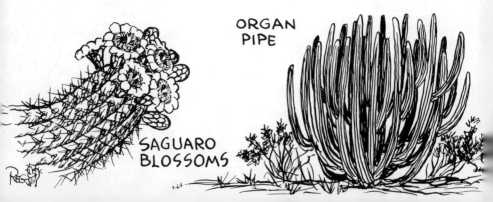

ORGAN PIPE

SAGUARO BLOSSOMS

The spidery branches of the organ pipe are a lot skinnier, and more numerous than those of its big brother, and the full grown plant is about half as tall. Pitahaya fruit is also palatable, and is harvested by the Papago Indians.

The organ pipe cactus is native to only one locality in the U.S., an area included, for the most part, within the borders of Organ Pipe National Monument, south of Ajo, along the Mexican border. And you'll find it growing in profusion in old Mexico, a few miles south of Nogales.

## DESERT WATER BARREL

The barrel cactus, or *bisnaga* (beez-NAH-gah — Spanish for barrel) seldom grows more than waist high, and at first glance you may mistake it for a small saguaro. It has similar accordion ridges, but you can quickly tell the difference by its thorns. Saguaro thorns are straight "needles", but the barrel cactus is armed with large, flat spikes, often red or yellow in color, with vicious hooks at the end. These tough curved spines interlace around the plant, forming a protective mesh which is hard for human hands or animal snout to penetrate.

The barrel has been widely heralded as a source of water for people lost on the desert, though some authorities contend that its juice is too brackish for human consumption. Judging from what some humans pay money to consume, this may be debatable. If you had anything stout enough to hack off the top of an average plant, the pulp could be beat up to squeeze out a quart or so of liquid. Whether or not a human stomach could stand it, we'd certainly not recommend it for filling your radiator. (Seriously, never drive across the desert without taking along several gallons of water. In case of car trouble, it's no fun to be without water, even for a short time.)

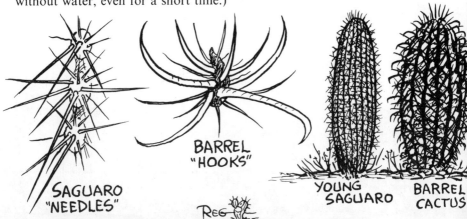

SAGUARO "NEEDLES"

BARREL "HOOKS"

REG

YOUNG SAGUARO

BARREL CACTUS

# JUMPERS AND PRICKLIES

The jumping cactus has the worst reputation of any desert plant, but actually it is the most affectionate, or at least the one to which you can become most attached on short acquaintance. It's the most innocent looking member of a large family of cacti, called *cholla* (CHAW-yuh), probably the most stickery clan of the desert. "Jumping" cactus is a misnomer — it can't hop an inch on its own power. But if you so much as brush against a cholla, its needles, covered with silky sheaths which look as soft as thistle down, fasten themselves to flesh like steel to a magnet. When cholla thorns make contact, it is the victim who jumps. But, finding himself yards away from the plant, with a segment of the cactus attached to his anatomy, he'll swear it was the cholla, not himself which did the leaping.

Other less belligerent varieties of cholla are the large, tree-like "staghorn", and the "chain-fruit", the fruit of which never ripens, but grows in clusters, one upon another, until it breaks off of its own weight and takes root.

Prickly pear cacti, made up of disc-shaped segments, like pancakes joined together, will undoubtedly be the most familiar to you of all cactus plants. Varieties of prickly pears are native to every state in continental U.S. except Maine, Vermont, New Hampshire and Alaska. Of course species of prickly pears vary greatly in size, from little plants with discs no bigger than your ear, to huge growths with segments like giant hot water bottles. Nearly all the prickly pears produce edible fruit, some so good that they are grown and harvested commercially. Of course, if you are going to eat this kind of "pears", you'll have to be careful — you could get a tongue full of stickers.

# LOVELIFE OF THE YUCCA

Three desert plants often called "cactus" which aren't even related to cacti, or to each other, are the yucca, the century plant, and the ocotillo.

The *yucca* (U like in "truck") is a full fledged member of the enor-

"JUMPING"
CHOLLA

YUCCA
"LILY"

mous *lily* family, which includes not only your garden variety of lilies, but also such familiar plants as onions, scallions and garlic. Largest of the yuccas is the Joshua tree (see page 46) which sometimes grows 30 feet tall, certainly the largest lily you'll ever see. Familiar names for other smaller varieties of yucca are "Spanish Dagger" and "Spanish Bayonet". The "bayonet" leaves grow in a cluster, making the plant look like a dwarf palm tree. Each year it sends up a stalk, two to six feet high, with a large bouquet of creamy white flowers at the tip. The yucca blossom is the state flower of New Mexico.

The flowers of each of more than two dozen varieties of yucca must be pollinated by its own particular kind of moth. The moth gathers pollen from one yucca, deposits it in the flower of another, in which it lays its egg. The pollinated flower thus produces fruit, upon which the new-hatched yucca worm will feed. The pollen is too heavy to be carried by the wind, and other insects will not carry it, so the plant is dependent on its moth for life. With one or two exceptions, no moth of a particular variety of yucca will have anything to do with any other yucca. Therefore the moth is also dependent on its yucca for life.

## THE CENTURY PLANT

The popular name for the *agave* (ah-GAH-vy) is "century plant", so called because of the infrequency with which it blooms — once in 10 to 70 years, and only once in its lifetime. The family of century plants comes in a great variety of sizes. In old Mexico, where it is called *maguey* (m'GAY) and *mescal* (mace-KAL), plants grow as high as a man, with broad leaves, cruelly pointed at the tip, and edged with sharp spines. They have plantations where century plants are cultivated to produce such potent Mexican beverages as "pulque" and "tequila". Note — *mescal* drinks are NOT to be confused with low-cal diet beverages.

Century plants native to Arizona's desert are much smaller, with short leaves, growing

CENTURY
PLANT

GROWING
FLOWER
STALK

in a rosette close to the ground — they look for all the world like huge artichokes. Once the century plant starts the blossoming process, it wastes no time. The flower stalk grows as much as a foot a day, looking like an overgrown asparagus shoot, until it is 15 to 30 feet high, topped by a festoon of pale yellow flowers. The result is beautiful, but the supreme effort so exhausts the plant that it withers and dies. However, this process is not quite as fatal as it sounds. During the maturing years, the plant produces many offshoots, so at time of death, it leaves heirs in various stages of development ready to carry on.

OCOTILLO BLOSSOM

## THE OCOTILLO

The ocotillo (oak-oh-TEE-yo), popularly known as the "monkey tail cactus" is another prime example of a "cactus" which is not a cactus at all. Actually it is a "fouquieria". And what is a "fouquieria"? Well now, after all, this is only a "popular priced" book, not a college course. But we can tell you, the ocotillo is one of the strangest, most beautiful of all desert plants. It is made up of spindly monkey-tail stems, 10 to 15 feet long, joined at the base, and fanned out like a peacock's tail. In rainy or humid weather these branches quickly put out rich green leaves to draw moisture from the air. When the atmosphere dries out, the ocotillo performs a quick strip tease, dropping all its leaves to cut down on evaporation of its water supply. Thorns which line each branch from tip to bottom, are hidden when the plant leafs out.

The ocotillo in bloom is a sight to behold. Each blossom is made up of scores of tiny, perfect bells, red as a stenographer's lipstick. They grow at the tip of each branch, like scarlet blow torch flames. An Arizona hillside in springtime, covered with blooming ocotillos is worth driving miles to see.

# DESERT TREES

There are cottonwoods and willows along the riverbeds of the Southwest, of course, but the true desert trees we have in mind are those which grow along the dry washes where the only water they ever see is from an occasional desert storm. These are the paloverde, mesquite, and ironwood, all members of the pea and bean family. Like all legumes, their seeds grow in pods.

In Spanish, paloverde (pal-oh-VAIR-day) means "green stick", and it is well named indeed. The paloverde is about the greenest tree you're ever likely to see. Everything about it, — the trunk, the branches, the twigs, the tiny leaves, and the large, sharp thorns — all are green. In springtime paloverde trees are covered with lemon-yellow, lacy blossoms that completely obscure the tree in a blaze of color. When the paloverde is in bloom, it dominates the whole color scheme of the desert.

Mesquite (m'SKEET) trees look like unpruned peach trees, except for their leaves, which are tiny, dull-green, and set in pairs along the stem, like little sprigs of fern. The sweet beans of the mesquite are favorites of cattle, rodents, even coyotes. Indians grind them into flour. Pioneers used tough mesquite wood for fence posts, and for tool handles. It was the number one fuel of the region before the coming of oil burners.

Ironwood looks a lot like mesquite, but the bark is a little grayer, the thorns are a little heavier, and the blossoms are purplish. The wood is much harder and heavier, too. So heavy, in fact, it will not float in water. It was never much use to early desert dwellers because they couldn't find tools tough enough to cut it.

(Editor's note: Of the host of plants that grow in Arizona's desert, we have described a few you may most readily pick out as you drive along. Tha'sall you're gonna get here, but for a more detailed treatise on desert flora, see the nice clerk who sold you this book, and invest in a copy of Reg Manning's "What Kinda Cactus Izzat?")

# WILD LIFE IN THE DESERT

Most people think of animal life in the desert as synonymous with poison, as in Gila (heela) Monsters, rattlesnakes and scorpions. You can spend a lifetime in Arizona without once seeing a Gila Monster outside a reptile garden. Hike through mountains and desert, and you may run across an occasional rattler, though they're not as plentiful here as in some other states. Scorpions are fairly common in communities bordered by desert areas. As civilization advances, and valleys are filled with people, the animals retreat further into the mountains, but there is still plenty of untamed life in the desert. Go out in the cactus country and sit quietly a while and at first you think the landscape is deserted. Then you start hearing the small hummings, chirpings, and rustlings of insects, birds, scurrying lizards, and other small animals. And you realize that the desert is teeming with life — and in an area where there isn't a sign of water. When paloverde and mesquite are in bloom, the trees will be in motion, as if fanned by an unseen breeze, which in fact they are — the fanning of a million tiny wings of bees.

Most populous communities of the desert are the great ant hills, so large that when they occur in irrigated fields, they're easily spotted from the air. The large red ants will ring their colonies with thorns from the "bullhead" plant, where available, to discourage you, in case you plan to tramp nearby in your bare feet.

Wherever you find a red ant hill, there's an excellent chance you may also find our favorite desert dweller, the horned toad. He's not really a toad, but a harmless and amusing little lizard, small enough to hold in your hand. However, he certainly is horned, with spikes around his head (like the Statue of Liberty's crown) and "thorns" on his body. Makers of horror-movies like to enlarge pictures of him a thousand times to represent a prehistoric dinosaur, and the effect is rather frightening. In real life he's fearsome only to the ants, which he gorges upon.

HORNED TOAD

DESERT CANTEEN

When you stroke his head with your finger, he'll close his eyes and seem to sleep.

You're not likely to see much of desert animals during the heat of day. Most of them come out after dark. And nearly all the desert dwellers can get along entirely without drinking water. The jackrabbit, which abounds (and bounds) in the dry country, dines on mesquite leaves and prickly pears. The succulent cactus pads not only provide forage, but enough moisture so the jack doesn't find it necessary to go out of his way looking for water.

Other desert rodents, cottontails, ground squirrels, and pack rats all get their moisture from prickly pears, cactus fruit and roots. But the kangaroo rat, a little guy with long hind legs, who bounds along at 10 feet per jump, has almost over-adjusted to the waterless life — he doesn't even care for water when it's available. He won't even eat succulent plants that are too juicy. And when he needs a bath, he goes out and dusts himself in a pile of sand.

Another animal which enjoys munching prickly pears is the javelina (hah-vay-LEAN-ah), or peccary, tough little "wild pig" of the desert. He digests stickers and all without discomfort. He also enjoys barrel cactus fruit, but has a healthy respect for the barrel's thorny armor. However, if he finds one of these plants which has tilted over, he will attack it from the unprotected underside, and completely hollow out its juicy interior.

## DESERT BIRDS

The Southwest desert abounds with bird life, but we'll only introduce you to a few varieties which are especially identified with this area.

THE CACTUS WREN is Arizona's state bird, largest member of the wren family, brownish in color, with spotted throat on breast, brown cap, and long white "eyebrow" markings. It builds its nest in cacti, the thornier the better, preferably jumping cholla. In fact, it

CACTUS WREN

always builds several nests, a main nest, and three or four replicas — which is confusing for its enemies, and bird photographers. The nests are covered, hollow-ball construction, the interior lined with any soft material available. Entry is through a narrow tunnel — try to stick your hand in and you may find it filled with cactus needles.

THE GILA WOODPECKER makes its nest, not just in, but inside the cacti — a small cavern, hollowed out inside a Giant saguaro. Those holes you see in almost every saguaro are the doorways of woodpecker apartments. The Gila woodpecker's back and wings have zebra black-and-white striping, with brownish body and head, and just a dab of red on the forehead. If the face you see staring at you from a wood-pecker's hole, has round eyes, and a very short beak, it will not be a woodpecker who has worn his bill to a nub. It will be a little owl.

THE ELF OWL is a miniature, no bigger than a fat sparrow, and it loves to move into vacated woodpecker cactus apartments, ready made, and comfortably cooled by surrounding watery pulp. And when the elf owl moves out, other birds are always ready to move in — there's seldom a "vacancy" sign on woodpecker-built lodgings.

THE ROADRUNNER is another desert bird who likes to nest in a cactus, or perhaps, a paloverde tree. He (or she) is a big bird, with topknot, a sharp, two-inch beak, and extremely long tail, which he uses as a rudder, fin, and stabilizer, while sprinting through the desert at greyhound speed. When he runs, his head, back and tail are extended in an arrow-straight line, till he throws the tail straight up, using it as a brake for sudden stops. The roadrunner can fly, but usually only to reach a tree top, from which he can glide long distances. The way he tilts his head, swings his tail, and dashes about, gives him a comic appearance, but he's actually a pretty tough character, well able to take care of himself in the rough and tumble battle of life. The fact that he is not above dining on other birds' eggs has given him a kind of bad reputation, but the roadrunner isn't really mean — he's just hungry.

If you're small enough to swallow, he may eat you, but entirely without malice. He will attack and kill a medium sized rattlesnake, not because he hates rattlers, but because he "likes" them. He also likes all kind and sizes of insects — and he dearly loves to snack on little lizards, which he scoops up at lightning speed.

THE TURKEY BUZZARD is the one bird you are certain to see if you drive through the Southwest desert. He's an American vulture, who gets his name from the fact that his head is nearly naked, wrinkled, and red, like the Thanksgiving bird. He's the garbage man of the desert, cleaning up after other animals — a messy business which doesn't endear him to those it benefits. On the ground he's not a lovely creature, and his takeoff is clumsy looking. But once air-borne, on wings spread their full five feet, soaring and wheeling, as he rides the desert air currents, nothing is more graceful, more beautiful. A desert landscape would not look right, somehow, without those black gliders endlessly circling off in the distance.

THE GAMBEL QUAIL is just about our favorite desert bird. It travels in coveys, and the family group of father, mother, and chicks marches single file through the creosote bush and mesquite. The Gambel quail will fly, if startled, but prefers to scurry around on foot. Both mom and pop have jaunty topknot feathers, but dad's is a little longer, and his plumage is a little gayer. She has bluish-gray feathers, and light tan breast, while he has a reddish brown cap, circled by a band of white, a black weskit, and a jet black throat, with an encircling band of white, from eye to eye.

# CROSSING ARIZONA'S SOUTHLAND

Heading west from Lordsburg, N.M., two routes cross Arizona's great desert and famous "winter playground" country: by way of U.S. 70, through Phoenix, to Blythe, California, and on to Los Angeles; or via U.S. 80 to Tucson, where you can also turn off to Phoenix, or continue west to Yuma, and on to San Diego. U.S. 80 follows the old Butterfield Stage route, about which more later.

Just inside the Arizona line, on U.S. 70, is the pleasant little cattle shipping center of Duncan. Take time to stop at the Art Gallery Drugstore, and look at the paintings of Hal Empie, druggist-artist-cartoonist, who may be mixing prescriptions, or oil colors, in the back of the store. His paintings are exhibited nationally, and millions of his "Kartoon-Kards" have been sold throughout the Southwest.

At Safford, 39 miles further west, you encounter one of those curious sets of contrasts so typical of Arizona. Here you can almost literally stand with your feet in hot water and your head in the snow. Mount Graham, which at altitude 10,717, is frosty topped much of the year, and cool at the summit even in midsummer, while at its base, the cities of Safford and Thatcher bask in their warm, irrigated valley. At Indian Hot Springs resort, northwest of Safford, hot water bubbles out of the ground at 119 degrees the year 'round. The mountain top, only a few miles from the valley below, via the Swift Trail, is a favorite retreat for vacationers and sportsmen. There's fishing at Riggs Lake. Deer and wild turkey inhabit the timbered slopes, which are part of the National Forest.

If the Gov'ment has a few billion bucks lying around that aren't committed for Europe or Asia or other water projects, we'd kinda like to have it devote some of them to looking into Arizona's hot water. We suspect there may be a boiling river running clear across the state, somewhere beneath U.S. 70 and 80. Hot water not only bubbles out of the ground at Indian Hot Springs, but also at Clifton, at Buckhorn Springs, near Mesa, and at Agua Caliente (Spanish for "hot water") west of Gila Bend.

Place names near Indian Hot Springs, Ft. Thomas and Geronimo, remind that U.S. 70 is about to cross the San Carlos Apache Reservation (pages 59-60) where pioneer travelers were kept in another kind of hot water by native "greeters". You may stop at the small Apache Arts and Crafts store at Bylas.

If you have time to drive an extra dozen miles, you may want to leave U.S. 70 just west of Bylas, and take the alternate route to Globe, via Coolidge Dam.

## COOLIDGE DAM

This is the world's largest multiple dome dam, entirely different from any other dam you're likely to see. It is formed by three huge concrete half-domes, 250 feet high, wedged in a canyon of the Gila River. From the lake side it looks like three baldheaded giants with everything submerged but their glistening pates. From the front it's a beautiful dam, with two giant spread-winged sculptured eagles as decorations between the arches, and the powerhouse nestled beneath the central dome.

San Carlos Lake, backed up behind the dam, provides excellent bass fishing. There are ramps for launching your boat, and you may rent boats, but there are no improved camp grounds. The reservoir furnishes water for the Casa Grande Valley, which includes the vast irrigated domain of the Pima Indians. The Pimas were traditional enemies of the Apaches, so it probably provided them some up-the-sleeves chuckles when rising waters of the artificial lake forced abandonment of the old Apache agency settlement of San Carlos. The tribal headquarters was moved to the old town of Rice, which became the "new" San Carlos. To reach it, turn off at Peridot on U.S. 70, and drive five miles north.

## GLOBE-MIAMI COPPER COUNTRY

Globe and Miami are so closely related in geography and interests, that they are usually referred to with a hyphen. The district is one of the richest copper producing areas the world has ever known. On the edge of Miami, bare white and ochre bluffs, rising steeply beside the

COOLIDGE
DAM'S
BALD HEADED MEN

highway, are clearly not works of nature. The land has the look of having been turned inside out, and that's exactly what happened here. These are old ore tailings, dumped here years ago, after minerals had been extracted from the earth. Today at open pit mines, dikes are built to retain the waste from worked out ore, and native shrubs and cacti are planted beside the dikes to hide the landscape's scars.

A short drive "up the hill" to Inspiration will provide you an unforgettable look at mines, smelters, leaching plants — the complete copper producing complex. Tours are conducted regularly for visitors — take plenty of film.

Globe and Miami form a highway hub. U.S. 60 comes in from the north, to join U.S. 70; Rte. 77 goes south toward Tucson, through more rich copper country around Hayden and San Manuel; the famous Apache Trail swings northwest; and U.S. 60-70 makes its scenic climb westward over the mountains and down to Superior, and on to Phoenix.

The descent into Superior is through Queen Creek Canyon, superb highway blasted out of the sheer cliffs — it's one of the most beautiful short stretches of road in the state. At Superior the rich and very deep underground mines produce silver and other valuable metals as well as copper. Superior is located at the base of the mountains that (Apaches say) once wept bitter tears.

## APACHE LEAP

From Superior's main street you can plainly see the granite cliffs atop which, legend says, a band of Apache warriors were cut off by a large enemy force (Spaniards, maybe?). With the sheer drop at their backs, they fought desperately, until their arrows were gone, and they faced capture. Rather than surrender, every Apache in the party leaped over the precipice. And the mountain wept molten tears — tears which hardened into drops of obsidian, and which strew the ground to this day.

A MIAMI COPPER MINE

Beds of perlite, volcanic material, near the base of the mountain, are filled with imbedded "Apache tears", obsidian nodules, adored by rock hounds. Just west of town, signs direct you to the "tear beds" where, for a small fee, you can gather your own droplets.

Three miles west of Superior you can see the boogum tree.

# DESERT GARDENS

The Boyce Thompson Southwestern Arboretum was founded by the late Col. Thompson, of Superior's Magma Copper Co., for research into the habits of plants that grow in sub-arid climates. Today the 1100-acre garden is operated by the University of Arizona. Here you'll see everything from roses to grasses, eucalyptus trees to wax-producing jojoba bushes, and cacti to the goofy little boogum tree. The boogum tree is related to the ocotillo and comes from Baja (Lower) California, in old Mexico. It looks like something out of a comic strip — like a huge white radish, planted upside down, with pointed top and spindly branches that look more like roots.

Fifty-five miles further west, U.S. 60-70 passes the Desert Botanical Garden of Arizona, in Papago Park, between Tempe and Phoenix. It is devoted entirely to growth and study of desert plants. Thousands of species of cacti and succulents from every corner of the globe may be seen here, growing outdoors in natural conditions. Other thousands of plants, in every stage of growth may be viewed in large lathhouses. You are permitted to take pictures, but stay on the paths. Some cacti are so small, one false step could wipe 'em out. Then, too, you might brush against a jumping cactus, and the staff is too busy to spend all afternoon removing stickers.

Scientists come from 'round the world to study plants at both these gardens — both are well worth visiting — and admission to both is free.

To see Arizona in its natural state, you can't beat the 30-mile stretch of U.S. 80-89 north of Tucson, between Oracle Jct. and Flor-

ence, known as the Pinal Pioneer Parkway. The Highway Department has acquired "scenic easements" beside the road, a band 1000 feet wide, in which this beautiful desert will be left just as Nature landscaped it. There are several rest areas, and signs identify the principal plants.

Fifteen miles east of Superior, and 16 miles north of Florence, U.S. 80-89 joins U.S. 60-70 at Florence Jct., and together they skirt the grim ramparts made famous by the Lost Dutchman.

## SUPERSTITION MOUNTAINS

There is a brooding beauty about the long range of mountains called "The Superstitions" — a kind of menacing grandeur that sends a little chill down your spine. For the Apaches, the Superstition Mountains are everything their name implies — a land of evil spirits. They shun it like a plague. But to the White Man it embodies the lure of *gold*. Somewhere, back among its crags, is the fabulous "Lost Dutchman Mine". Maybe.

Sometime during the 1870s, a white-bearded German prospector, named Jacob Walz, plodded out of the Superstitions to quench his thirst at the bars of the new little desert community of Phoenix. And he paid his way with gold. Many times he returned to the mountains to replenish his supply, and there were plenty who tried to follow, without success. Several who tracked him into the badlands, never came back. When the "Old Dutchman" died, the secret of his mine perished too.

Since his death, hundreds of people have sought the "Old Dutchman's" mine, but none have found it. Bleached skeletons testify to the danger that awaits the unwary in Superstitions' maze of canyons.

For years the Dons Club, of Phoenix, has conducted an annual "Lost Gold Trek" into the Superstitions, on a Sunday in March, to allow visitors to prospect for the Old Dutchman's treasure. So far the mountain has kept its secret.

The mysterious facade of the Superstitions forms a backdrop for Apache Junction, a thriving community built around an old crossroads, where U.S. 60-70-80-89 meet the Apache Trail. Here are the most modern accommodations, which often house movie crews filming in the beautiful desert nearby. In case you're worried about the haunting feeling you've been here before, it was probably only that you "saw it in the cinema."

## THE APACHE TRAIL

The Apache Trail is the result of evolution. Originally it was just what the name says, a trail used by Apache war parties retreating into the mountains after raids on habitations of the Salt River Valley. Signs along the modern trail point out plainly visible remnants of the old pony path. Later soldiers tracked the raiders into their stronghold, and the trail ran red. A sign indicates Apache Gap, scene of one bloody battle.

When Theodore Roosevelt Dam was built, a tortuous wagon road was constructed to freight in supplies. Roosevelt Dam is the largest masonry dam ever built. It rises 284 feet above bedrock, is 184 feet thick at the base, and 16 feet thick at its top. 343,000 cubic yards of stone were used, quarried from the nearby mountain-sides. A mill was built on the site, and all the cement used in the mortar, 338,000 barrels of it, was manufactured from clay and limestone deposits near the dam. When you look up at the enormous rock wall which is Roosevelt Dam, just remember that every ton of supplies, every bit of machinery had to be hauled into the canyon by wagon train. As you pilot your car over Apache Trail, try to imagine how it would be to "skin" a twenty-mule team, hauling barrels of crude petroleum, over the same route. Only in those days the trail was about half as wide as it is today.

Today the Apache Trail has been widened for motor traffic, though it's still no six-lane freeway. It's paved about half way from Apache

HAULING SUPPLIES
To BUILD
ROOSEVELT DAM

Junction to Roosevelt Dam, and all the way from the dam to Globe, but the most spectacular section of the trail is still gravel-surfaced. It is probably the safest road you'll ever travel, precisely for the reason that it doesn't look the least bit safe — it's one road where drivers pay strict attention to their driving. Most people, making the trip for the first time, where the curves have your steering wheel spinning like a raffle device, divide their comments about half and half between prayers for deliverance, and exclamations over the wild beauty.

Fish Creek Hill is the most hair raising point on the trail. The cliffs rise sheer on one side, and drop away hundreds of feet on the other. The roadway cut in the cliff face is really wide enough, but it seems like a pin scratch. The breathless feeling you get as you drive down, or up Fish Creek Hill is not caused by the altitude.

## DAMS OF THE SALT

September 20, 1906, the first stone of Theodore Roosevelt Dam, measuring four feet long, three feet wide, and ten inches chick, was cemented in place. The last stone was laid February 5, 1911, and Teddy himself dedicated the mighty structure March 18. The great concrete dams that have been built since are larger and higher, but somehow their "slick" look doesn't match the throat catching majesty of this awesome pile of stone. The federal government loaned $10,166,000 to build the dam, which has long since been paid back in full.

As you travel the Apache Trail, you will see lakes formed by three additional dams constructed in the Salt River below Roosevelt. They are Apache Lake, behind Horse Mesa Dam, Canyon Lake, back of Mormon Flat Dam, and Saguaro Lake, formed by Stewart Mountain Dam — lakes that supply water for irrigating the great Salt River Valley. And each of the dams provides hydro-electric power for farms, industry and residential use in the Phoenix metropolis and surrounding areas. The lakes are also favorite sites for boating, fishing, swim-

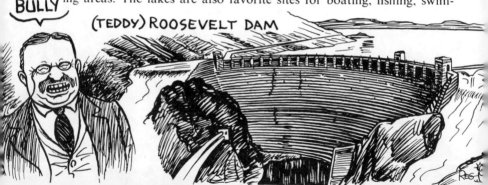

BULLY

(TEDDY) ROOSEVELT DAM

ming and just picnicking. The state Game and Fish Dept. keeps them well stocked, and the U.S. Forest Service supervises recreation areas.

Two other dams, Bartlett and Horseshoe, located on the Verde River, furnish supplemental storage, particularly for Phoenix drinking water. At the point where the Salt and Verde Rivers come together, Granite Reef Diversion Dam catches water released from reservoirs upstream, and channels it into the great network of canals in the valley.

Luckless raindrops that fall into the drainage area of the Salt River Valley irrigation system, are the hardest worked bits of water in the universe. As water passes through Roosevelt Dam, it has to turn the huge turbines in the power house — but that's only the beginning! After captivity in each lake, water escapes through succeeding power houses, only to be recaptured and put to work again. When it finally reaches the valley, through canals and ditches, and soaks into the fields, you'd think they'd let it go its weary way to the sea — but not so. They have hundreds of pumps all over the valley, which draw it back to the surface, pour it into the ditches, and make it go to work all over again. About the only escape is evaporation.

# TONTO CLIFF DWELLINGS

From the Apache Trail, 30 miles north of Globe, two ruins are plainly visible in their cliff niches. The turn-off sign directs you to Tonto National Monument, only a mile from the highway, where you may visit the cave dwellings. The "lower" ruin, 300 feet above the monument headquarters, is reached by a good half-mile zig-zag path. This prehistoric apartment house was originally two stories high and had 19 rooms, several of them "upstairs". The outside walls were broken down by vandals before the National Monument was established. The "upper" ruin is a mile and a half from the visitor center by trail. Because of the dry climate, artifacts uncovered from caved in rooms are in an excellent state of preservation, and may be seen at the monument museum. They reveal that the people were experts in the crafts of weaving, tool and pottery making. They made artistic

ROOSEVELT DAM

HORSE MESA DAM

MORMON FLAT DAM

STEWART MTN. DAM

DIVERSION DAM

GATE
MAIN CANAL
SIPHONS
SECONDARY CANAL
GATE
DITCH

IRRIGATION

jewelry from turquoise and shells. The shells were probably obtained from the Gulf of California, below Yuma.

Six hundred years ago, the old boy who sat on his porch, eating corn bread and sipping his cactus fruit-juice cocktail, while the little woman was weaving a new pair of yucca-leaf sandals, and while the kiddies were frolicking 'mongst the cacti on nearby slopes, had a glorious view of valley, river and mountains. But, more important, he could spot approaching enemies miles away, in ample time to prepare a reception. The steep slope, covered with loose slide-rocks and jumping cholla, made attacking the cliff houses from below a distinct non-profit enterprise. The overhang of the cliff provided protection from above.

Security, rather than gracious living, made it worth while to hike all the way down to the river in the valley below, where small brush dams in the river stored water to irrigate fields of corn, squash, beans and cotton. Sites of the little dams and the fields are now covered by the great reservoir of their huge modern successor, five miles downstream.

## PHOENIX UP FROM THE "ASHES"

One day in 1867, Jack Swilling, who made his living looking at the ground (he was a prospector) noticed something different about the ground as he rode through the valley of the Salt River. There were lots of mounds, and the ground around them was littered with bits of broken pottery. Nearby were remains of old ditches. The mounds were clearly crumbled ruins of ancient buildings, and the ditches were unmistakably part of a prehistoric irrigation system. Sometime in the past, Swilling reasoned, the valley had been inhabited by people who were skilled farmers — and very careless dish washers.

This gave Swilling an idea — if prehistoric Indians could irrigate the valley for farming, why not the modern settlers of 1867? He sold the idea to business men in the bustling mining camp of Wickenburg,

who put up $10,000 and organized a company to build a brush dam in the Salt River, enlarge some of the old ditches, and lay out a town. "This city will arise from the ashes of the past civilization like the fabled Phoenix bird," said "Lord" Darrel Duppa, an English remittance man, admired for his book larnin'. And so the new town of Phoenix had a name.

Within a year after the Swilling Irrigating Canal Co. went into action, several ranches had been established, crops harvested, and the first business building, Hancock's Store, was erected. The one-story 'dobe structure served as courthouse as well as store and butcher shop. (Customers cut off their own steaks, using their own knives, for two-bits a pound.) By 1872 the San Diego Union could report that Phoenix "contains many houses, stores, work shops, hotels, butcher shop, courthouse, jail and an excellent school." It went on to prophesy, "When it has become the capital city of the Territory, which it will, undoubtedly, at no very distant day, and when the 'iron horse' steams through our country. . .the Salt River Valley will be the garden of the Pacific Slope, and Phoenix the most important inland town."

The first "iron horse" steamed into Phoenix in 1887, and two years later it became the seat of the territorial government. The "iron horse" played its part in actually moving the legislature to the new capital city. The only direct route, via the old Black Canyon stage road, was not only rough, but it must have presented a problem to locate enough coaches to haul all the lawmakers at once. They chose the longer, but more comfortable way by rail from the old capital of Prescott, to Phoenix, via Los Angeles, and back through Yuma.

As you drive through the Salt River Valley today, you can see the fulfillment of Duppa's prediction — canals, rich farm land, Phoenix and its satellite cities, populated by almost a million people. And at Phoenix' municipally owned and excavated Pueblo Grande Ruin, you can see the old mounds, and remains of one of the prehistoric ditches.

UP FROM THE ASHES OF A
PREHISTORIC CIVILIZATION —

# HOHOKAM

The whole history of Europeans in the New World, from Columbus to today, spans less than five centuries. The prehistoric residents of central Arizona, the Hohokam, successfully and continuously operated irrigation systems in the great desert valleys for 17 centuries. Excavations of the Snaketown Ruins, near Chandler, directed by Arizona's noted archeologist, Dr. Emil Haury, prove that the Hohokam were irrigating their farms here as far back as 300 B.C. Their canals were dug with stone and wooden tools, but were superbly engineered. They made fine pottery, decorated with designs which became progressively more artistic through the ages. Unfortunately their culture dictated that when a person died, his pots must also "die" — therefore all that busted pottery. Using acetic acid, made from fermented saguaro cactus fruit, the Hohokam perfected the etching of designs on sea shells, 400 years before the process was invented by European armor makers.

(The ruins at Snaketown, on the Gila Indian Reservation of the Pimas, have been covered over to protect them till the site may be designated as a National Monument.)

There have been several theories about what caused the Hohokam (a Pima word for "vanished ones") to vanish. Perhaps the area became uninhabitable because of a great drouth, or conversely, because of waterlogging due to prolonged irrigation, or because of raiding by hostile tribes. Or maybe, after 17 centuries, they just got sick of the place. We have a theory of our own which seems logical. Everybody knows you can't go 'round building irrigation projects without the approval of the gov'ment in Washington. Right? Right! Y'gotta get a loan, organize power districts and all like that. The Hohokam didn't know this. They just built dams like the beavers, dug miles of ditches, and waited for rain. And the whole thing worked great. Then, one day, someone came along and told them the entire system was illegal without a gov'ment permit. But when they went looking for Washington,

HAS *WASHINGTON* OKAYED THIS IRRIGATION PROJECT?

D.C., to get the official okay, the financing, crop quotas, etc., they discovered that it hadn't been invented yet. This so discouraged and frustrated them, they smashed all their pots and walked away from it all.

# IN AND AROUND PHOENIX

In the phone book, at the local banks, or at the CofC, you can get info about things to see — theaters, museums, libraries, parks, golf courses, or current happenings like rodeos, concerts, etc., so we'll not try to list everything here. We'll just mention a few things you oughta look for.

CAMELBACK MOUNTAIN — northeast part of the city — nobody will have to point it out for you. It dominates the valley — Nature's sculpture of a reclining dromedary.

In Mesa, the MORMON TEMPLE — it's not a church in the usual sense — not every Mormon, even, is permitted to enter — only those who have most nearly lived up to rigid church ideals may be married, baptized, etc., in the Temple. But you can tour the grounds, with the building beautifully reflected in its mirror pond.

On Arizona State University campus in Tempe, visit GRADY GAMMAGE AUDITORIUM, named after the prexy who guided the school to university status, and famed as the last architectural masterpiece of the late great Frank Lloyd Wright. North of Scottsdale you may visit Taliesin West, where Wright lived and worked.

At the Heard Museum, ask to see the fabulous Barry Goldwater collection of KACHINA DOLLS. "LITTLE EMMA", Arizona's first locomotive, may be seen at the Arizona Museum.

At the Phoenix Art Museum, don't miss the superb collection of ancient CHINESE IVORY CARVINGS.

At the Desert Botanical Garden in Papago Park, near Tempe, look for the crazy BOOGUM TREE, and the TOTEM POLE CACTUS, which looks like it was made of wax, which has melted in the hot sun.

CAMELBACK MTN.

At South Mountain Park (they say this is the nation's largest city park) take the paved drive to the top, where several VIEW-POINTS give you tremendous views of the valley. If you ride or hike over the 40 miles of trails, look for the excellent PREHISTORIC PICTURE WRITING.

In the spring, visit the JAPANESE FLOWER GARDENS, along Baseline Road — spectacular fields of blossoms.

Near Chandler visit the SPRECKELS SUGAR FACTORY — it's almost magic how they can take huge white sugar beets, and convert them into sugar crystals, with any size of granules that they desire.

# WICKENBURG

The town which grubstaked founders of modern Phoenix is still there, 55 miles northwest of the state capital. It owes its own founding to a prospector's runaway burro. The burro belonged to ol' Henry Wickenburg, who was looking for precious metals back in 1863, in the mountains southwest of the present town. Though it was no new experience to have his pack animal take time out for a little side trip, Henry never enjoyed chasing his long-eared companion through the chaparral. This time the prospector was all out of patience by the time he caught up with the burro. Buzzards circled hopefully overhead as he stooped to pick up a handful of rocks — there was always the chance that the angry man might carry out his oft-voiced threats to murder his ornery critter.

Wickenburg's first rock whizzed harmlessly past a long ear, which waggled disdainfully. Henry recalculated his range, direction, and windage, and set himself to launch another missile — but the second stone was never hurled. In it the old miner's practiced eye had detected a long sought gleam — the gleam of gold!

Did Henry Wickenburg name his gold mine after the burro? Nope. He named it the Vulture Mine, after the disappointed buzzards. Was it a rich strike? Well, before it was through the mine produced $10 million in gold. But it was not "finders-keepers" for Henry — "bad investments and sharpers" took most of his fortune. On the banks of the Hassayampa River, 12 miles from the mine, Wickenburg was founded as a mill town to handle the ore. There's a legend which says anyone who drinks of the Hassayampa's waters shall never speak the truth — which may give rise to a slight credibility gap concerning the story of Henry's burro. But there really was a Henry Wickenburg, and a Vulture Mine, and there really is a town of Wickenburg. Today it's the famed "Guest Ranch Capital".

Guest registers of Wickenburg's "dude" ranches list names of people from all over the world who come to enjoy life in the saddle. The atmosphere is rustic, but life is exceedingly comfortable at these fine ranches — except for time spent aboard horses, which admittedly has its areas of discomfort for tenderfeet. Occasionally "dude" wranglers, cowboy "pros" employed by the ranches, will stage small rodeos at the various spreads, to demonstrate their skill atop the cayuses.

Each April Wickenburg's Desert Caballeros conduct Arizona's oldest "ride" for 200 horsemen who come from more than half of the 50 states, including an annual contingent from Alaska. The long line of riders parade out of town on a Monday morning, and return five days later. During the week they cover trails once traveled by explorers and prospectors, through wild and beautiful country where pioneers rode only at the risk of losing their scalps. One day of the ride is spent at a big encampment, with trapshooting, rodeos, and racing. Nights are around the campfire, with typical cowboy entertainment.

West of Wickenburg, on U.S. 60, you'll see a roadside monument marking the scene where stagecoach passengers were massacred by an Indian war party. (There wouldn't be room to mark spots along the highways where travelers have been massacred by "civilized" motorists). Westward, U.S. 60 and Rte. 72 continue to the Colorado River, and its lower lakes (page 42-43).

Twenty-four miles northwest of Wickenburg is the start of the Joshua Tree Parkway, which extends 17 miles along U.S. 93, on the way to Kingman and Hoover Dam (page 47). Fifty-nine miles north of Wickenburg via U.S. 89 (97 miles from Phoenix, via the Black Canyon route) is Arizona's first territorial capital.

# PRESCOTT

December 29, 1863, the first governor, John N. Goodwin, proclaimed Arizona a territory and added this note, "The seat of government will for the present be at or near Fort Whipple." Since there was no town "at or near" the fort, a new one was built, using logs from pines at the site. They named it Prescott, after a famous historian of the time. Most pretentious structure in the new community was the two-story "governor's mansion", which cost a whopping (in that day) $6000. It did double duty as the meeting place of Arizona's First Territorial Legislature, before a capitol was built. The old log "mansion" still stands, a part of the Sharlot Hall Museum, named after the poet, historian, and gracious lady who was principally responsible for preserving it. She also collected many of the relics of pioneer life displayed there, including the first governor's chair. Today Fort Whipple, the old frontier post, is a Veteran's Administration Hospital.

Overlooking the first capital city, from a hill at the base of Thumb Butte, is the Arizona Pioneers Home. The men and women who live here, our state's first citizens, can remember territorial days, when it took their horse-drawn vehicles a full day to negotiate the distance we travel in half an hour on modern freeways.

GOV. GOODWIN

FIRST GOVERNOR'S MANSION

Prescott claims that its Frontier Days cowboy festival, held July 4th, 1888, was the world's first rodeo. It has been staged every year since then, and is still one of the state's principal Independence Day celebrations.

Step into any store in Prescott and the chances are you may meet a man who has had a live snake in his mouth at least once during the past year. Prescott is the home of the "Smoki" people, White citizens banded together to study and preserve the ways of the Indian. One of their "courses of study" is the Hopi Snake Dance, which requires very intimate handling of reptiles. However, Smokis wisely refrain from using rattlesnakes for research. The annual Smoki Ceremonial, certainly one of America's most unusual shows, is presented the second Sunday in June. Behind the anonymity of authentic costumes and paint, the dedicated business men of Prescott achieve surprisingly realistic interpretations of Indian dances.

# ROUTE OF THE STAGE COACHES

Hardly a trace remains of Arizona's old stage stations, but you'll be closely following the route of the old Butterfield Overland Mail when you cross Arizona from Lordsburg, N.M., to Yuma, via Interstate 10 and 8 through Tucson.

In 1857 the San Antonio and San Diego Stage Co. started the first regular stage service between Texas and California. Financing was provided by a federal mail contract for $149,000 to make up the difference between actual cost of carrying a letter across the continent ($65) and the cost of a stamp (10c). Sample passenger fares: San Diego to Ft. Yuma, $40; to Tucson $80; to San Antonio, $200. Passengers were "GUARANTEED to ride in Coaches, excepting 180 miles" — the 180 miles across the desert between Ft. Yuma and San Diego, which was by mule back. This led to nicknaming the line the "Jackass Mail".

While the Jackass Mail was working on actual operations of its stage line, one Mr. John Butterfield was working in Washington, D.C.,

to get a new mail contract from Congress. He got it — $600,000 a year to provide twice-a-week service from St. Louis to San Francisco. The original line lost its subsidy — and went out of business. So you thought maybe federal subsidies and influences on private enterprise started with the New Deal?

Mr. Butterfield's Overland Mail turned out to be a first rate stage line, with 750 employees, 100 coaches, and 1500 horses and mules. The emphasis was on speed, with the almost 2800 miles between Missouri and San Francisco usually being covered in 23 days. Once, with the aid of a following wind, and following Apaches, they made it in the record time of 16 days. At each of some two dozen stops in the 437-mile stretch across Arizona, fresh six-horse teams would be harnessed and waiting as the stage rolled in. Five minutes was allowed to change teams, but at "meal stations" the stop was for 20 minutes — ample time to consume the feast of jerky, beans and coffee. Cost of the meal, 40c to a dollar — no tip.

Passengers were asked to bring along "1 Sharp's rifle, and 100 cartridges, 1 Colt's revolver and 2 pounds of balls, a knife and a pair of blankets". In addition each passenger was allowed 30 pounds of luggage, which it was suggested should include "1 pair of thick boots, 6 pairs woolen socks, woolen pants, 6 undershirts, 3 woolen shirts, 1 wide-awake hat, a cheap sack coat, a soldier's overcoat, 1 pair gauntlets, 3 or 4 towels, and a small oil bag of needles, pins, sponge, hair brush, comb, and soap." (What? No deodorant or mouth wash?)

The rifle and revolver were not for ornament. In case of attack a passenger might well have to protect himself — this was Apache country. The company established a gifts-for-Apaches policy which held attacks on coaches to a minimum. Apparently this informal "protection racket" did not apply to horse stealing, though — losses of stock in Indian raids was a major item of expense.

Local feeder stage lines sprang into existence connecting outlying Arizona communities with the Butterfield main line. The stage coach business was off and rolling in a big way — then the Civil War broke out. In 1861 Confederates in Texas confiscated Butterfield stock and property. U.S. troops were pulled out of Arizona. Left without protection and with no place to go, the Overland Mail was folded up, personnel and equipment were withdrawn to California, and stations were abandoned and burned. For ten years the territory was practically cut off from the outside world. In the early 1870's a Texas to California stage line was put in service, but as the railroads grew, it shrunk. Finally rails extended all the way, and the stage line disappeared. However, the feeder stage routes continued in operation right on into the 20th Century, until the coming of the motor bus.

Probably the most history-packed spot on the old Butterfield route was Apache Pass, 15 miles south of the town of Bowie. The ruins of old Fort Bowie and the stage station in the pass have been designated a National Historic Site, but access roads and other development work are not yet completed, and at this writing it is a primitive area. (Inquire at nearby Chiricahua National Monument.)

## COCHISE

Cochise county, which occupies the southeast corner of Arizona, is named after the greatest of all Apache chieftains. The famous chief was on good terms with Americans until a fateful day in 1860 when, accompanied by four of his braves, he was visiting American friends at Apache Pass. An overzealous 2nd Lt. Bascom ordered them seized and charged with depredations actually committed by a renegade band of Indians. Cochise promptly escaped, but, on orders of young Bascom, his four tribesmen were hanged — an injustice which was to cost hundreds of American and Apache lives. During the ensuing dozen years Cochise raided ranches and settlements, ambushed army detach-

ments, spreading terror everywhere. One of the biggest battles was fought at Apache Pass, where the Apaches took on the famous California Column, and were driven off only by army howitzers.

It was at this time in history that Tom Jeffords picked to establish a stage line between Ft. Bowie and Tucson. Apaches killed 22 of his men in 16 months, so Jeffords tried an audacious maneuver. He rode alone into Cochise's Stronghold for a face to face appeal to the fierce chief. To fully appreciate Jefford's bravery you must realize that he had a bushy red beard, and a matching head of hair that would have made an enviable addition to any scalp collection. Cochise so admired "Red Whiskers' " courage that a lifelong friendship sprang up, culminating in a ceremony which made them "blood brothers". Tom Jeffords' stages were never molested again.

In 1872 President Grant sent Gen. O. O. Howard to make peace with Cochise, and Tom Jeffords was called upon to bring them together. A treaty was signed, but not until Cochise was assured that Jeffords would be made Indian Agent of a new reservation. When the old chieftain died two years later, Jeffords was the only white man allowed to know the location of his grave — a secret he never revealed. It is somewhere in Cochise Stronghold, now a State Recreation Area in the Dragoon Mts., 10 miles west of U.S. 666, south of Willcox.

Almost in the shadow of the Chiricahua Mts. at the little town of Apache, near the New Mexico line on U.S. 80, is a roadside marker commemorating the surrender of a later, more infamous Apache.

## GERONIMO

This notorious Apache medicine man was bad medicine for all Whites and a particular headache to the War Department. He was a reservation Indian who felt that life as a ward of the government did not fulfill his needs. He wanted to get into the cattle business and engage in foreign trade. So he ran away from the reservation, scalped

COCHISE AND "RED WHISKERS"

local ranchers, stole their stock and traded them across the border in Mexico. And vice versa. The border proved very convenient in Geronimo's business. When soldiers got too hot on his trail, he simply skipped across the line and thumbed his nose.

When business was slack, Geronimo would allow himself to be captured and returned to the reservation, where he could rest and recruit new followers. As soon as the easy life palled, he would strike out on another raiding party. We have had gangsters in modern times who seemed to have no more trouble getting "out of jail" as frequently as Geronimo, but in one respect the Indian's escapes were different — he relied on his own wits, not legal manipulation to get "sprung".

In 1886 Geronimo gave himself up for the last time. As a reward, the Gov'ment sent him for a tour of Florida, Alabama and Oklahoma — all expenses paid.

A favorite hideout for followers of Cochise and Geronimo was the Chiricahua range, southeast of Willcox, north of Douglas, and within easy striking distance of Apache Pass. At the northern end of the range is an extravagant example of Nature's prowess as a sculptor.

# WONDERLAND OF ROCKS

Nature had a nightmare — and at Chiricahua National Monument you see the result — 16,000 acres of weird stone figures, carved by countless centuries of wind and rain. Chiricahua is pronounced chee-ree-CAH-wah — or "cheery-cow" in colloquial Spanish. It is usually referred to locally as the "Wonderland of Rocks", which is no exaggeration.

You drive into the Wonderland between long tiers of stony-faced giants that make you feel like an ant crawling up the aisle of some fantastic temple. But you quickly pass through this first group and climb out of sight around the mountain, to come out a few minutes later at a higher up vantage point and parking area, seven miles from

GERONIMO

the Monument Visitor Center. From here 16 miles of well constructed trails lead to every major attraction. Outstanding is the "duck", which is really a good image of the complete bird.

Most of the stone figures are in the shape of columns surmounted by larger knobs or "heads". In many cases the columns have worn so thin at their "necks" that wind pressure has split them, leaving the heads actually separated from the body, but neatly balanced atop the "shoulders". One such head is as big as a house, and weighs more than two million pounds. Yet it balances on a point little larger than the seat of your overstuffed chair. And it sways gently in the wind.

Near the parking lot, one of the rocks has been converted into an iron railed observation tower. From this "pulpit" you have a view of the whole vast "congregation" spread out below and all around. Nearby you can visit a geological exhibit.

To the northeast, clearly discernable on the skyline is "Cochise Head", the upturned profile of the famous chief formed by the 8,100 foot high silhouette of the Chiricahua Mts. A beautiful side trip, for those who don't mind narrow, unsurfaced mountain roads, is the route over the Chiricahuas between the National Monument and Rodeo, N.M. It takes you through heavily timbered altitudes of Rustlers Park and beautiful Cave Creek Canyon. Snow usually closes the road in winter.

## DOUGLAS AND BISBEE

The southern terminous of U.S. 666 at the Mexican border is Douglas. "Across the street" is the little Mexican town of Agua Prieta, where you can get those souvenirs — anything from hand carved canes to Mexican tequila. Douglas is the gateway to the Mexican big game country, famed for its leopard-spotted jaguar. The principal thing at Douglas is the great smelter which gets its ore from the Lavender Pit, 24 miles away at Bisbee.

"CHEERY COW" WONDERLAND

Bisbee's Main Street is the paved floor of a canyon. The buildings and houses cling to the steep canyon sides. In some places, the rise is so sharp that curbs are four or five feet high on one side of the street. Bisbee has had its share of wild and woolly history. The very name of "Brewery Gulch" has a swing that only the old timers knew how to get into their nomenclature. Probably the outstanding gun fight in Bisbee history was the Castenada Store holdup and killing in 1884, which resulted in dramatic justice being meted out to the bandits involved. They were taken to Tombstone, then the county seat, and all five of them were hanged simultaneously from a specially built gallows.

If you didn't get your souvenirs in Agua Prieta, you can get them at Naco, across the Mexican border, a few minutes drive from Bisbee.

# FORT HUACHUCA

This old army fort, 25 miles from Bisbee, was established in 1887, and became one of the principal outposts during the days of the Apache outbreaks. During hectic days in Mexico, it served to guard the border. Several times it was almost abandoned, but a bill to decommission it could never be drawn up — lawmakers couldn't spell it. To pronounce it is tough enough — you sneeze it, "wah-CHOO-kah". During World War II it became a huge troop training center. Today it is one of the nation's most important U.S. military electronic testing centers.

# TOMBSTONE

It was at Ft. Huachuca that Ed Schieffelin resigned his job as a frontier army scout, to go prospecting. "Hell, all you'll ever find out there is yore tombstone, Ed!" they told him as he started his solo trek through the Apache infested hills toward the Dragoon Mts. But Schieffelin found silver — a fabulous mine. The town that mushroomed into existence took the name of Tombstone.

While the mines held out, Tombstone was the rip roaringest town the West has known. It used to be the first duty of the man who opened

HUACHUCA!

GESUNDHEIT!

up for business each morning, to sweep the bodies off the board walk in front of his store. One never crossed the street without looking right and left to make sure a bullet was not coming. The mines scarcely did more excavation than the undertaker (who would have shot you if you'd called him a "mortician"). This gent with the black crepe bedecked high hat, furnished two classes of service: the class B "tourist" burial; and the First Class De Luxe, which included removing the boots. Today you can visit Tombstone's old Boot Hill graveyard (definitely no "memorial garden") where they planted the remains of notorious bad men, at least one lynch victim, the mass-execution quintet from Bisbee, and assorted innocent bystanders.

And you can visit the famous "Bird Cage". What a glorious place the old Bird Cage was. This rich and rowdy town, of 15,000 population, could and did lay enough cash on the line to attract the finest actors from San Francisco and New York. Of course they all played at the Bird Cage Theater. There was a bar in the theater, almost as long as the stage. Square box stalls lined the walls. Seats on the main floor were movable, so that they could be pushed aside after the performance, to allow the show girls to come out and dance with the audience.

The old County Courthouse in Tombstone is now a museum. Over by the O.K. Corral you can walk the ground where the Earps, assisted by Doc Holliday, fought it out in the street with the Clantons — perhaps the most famous gun battle of all time. And down the street is the office of the old Tombstone Epitaph — it took courage to run a newspaper in those days. The Epitaph is still being published — a copy of the paper will make a swell souvenir.

The end of Tombstone's mining prosperity came, not as the result of running out of ore, but, paradoxically for an Arizona community, because of too much water. An underground stream so strong and endless that it flooded all the mines in the vicinity literally drowned the

boomtown. We still think the water starved West could make use of all that underground water, but pumping proved far too expensive for any of the mines to carry on.

Tombstone was "too tough to die" and lives on as a place where you can rub shoulders with the past. High on a hill, overlooking the town, is a 20-foot stone monument. It is Ed Schieffelin's tombstone.

## PADRE KINO

For a century and a half after Coronado's fruitless search for the golden streets of Cibola (page 63) the usual format for Spanish expeditions through Arizona was for two or three priests to be escorted by a couple of hundred soldiers. This was not always a happy arrangement for the priests, since the soldiers tended to be more interested in looking for precious metal than in saving Indian souls. In the case of the Fray Rodriquez Expedition of 1580, the soldiers discovered silver along the Gila River, and forgot their hapless padre altogether — he was killed by Apaches.

In 1691 Padre Eusebio Francisco Kino made his first trip to southern Arizona, part of his new parish of "Pimeria Alta", 50,000 square miles which included a large chunk of the present Mexican state of Sonora. Before his death in 1711, Father Kino thoroughly explored and mapped this Southwest region as far west as Yuma, and as far north as the Casa Grande Ruins, which he discovered. Among the many missions he founded were San Xavier and Tumacacori, in Arizona, and among the "ranches" he established for friendly Pimas and Papagos was one at today's site of Tucson. He stocked the ranches with cattle and taught the Indians to grow and store the grain to feed them. Padre Kino's maps of the area were not improved upon for a hundred years, the good that he did in a comparatively brief time has seldom been equaled in history.

# TUMACACORI MISSION

"Too-mah-COCK-oh-ree" sounds like an Indian discussing the results of a Mexican cock fight, but it's actually the way you pronounce Tumacacori. Through the years the mission increased in importance, but founding Father Kino never saw the present building which wasn't started until about 1800. It took 20 years to build, and still was never really finished. But you must realize that the builders had to make their own bricks (some fired) from clay right on the grounds, and the padres were using strictly non-union Indian labor. Nevertheless the interior was decorated, and the mission was opened for worship. But not for very long.

In 1821 Mexico declared its independence, and financial support for missions from Spain was cut off. Parishes were required to support their own churches, and Mexico began ordering the missionaries out of the frontiers. Tumacacori's priest was withdrawn in 1828, though services were held there occasionally until 1849 when the Indians abandoned it. Weather and vandals reduced it to ruins.

Today it is a National Monument. The complete desolation of ruin has been cleaned up, and parts of the building, such as tumbled roofs, etc., have been restored. But the Park Service has done nothing to mar the atmosphere of antiquity. We know of no place that can get under your hide like Tumacacori. Inside the massive 'dobe walls and beneath the great sanctuary dome is a little section of the world that seems to have stopped where it stood centuries ago.

# TUBAC

Three miles north of Tumacacori on U.S. 89 is the little "town with nine lives". Tubac has died eight times, but is now very much alive again. In 1752, following an uprising of the Pima Indians, Spanish soldiers established a "presidio" (garrison) at Tubac. Many citizens of San Francisco, California, may be surprised to learn that this tiny

community in Arizona is their parent city. It was here that Capt. Juan Bautista de Anza, commander of the presidio, put together an expedition of 240 colonists and trekked to the Golden Gate, where he founded the presidio and mission of San Francisco in 1776. In San Francisco's first census, one of every three residents recorded Tubac as their birthplace.

Through the centuries Tubac has been abandoned, or wiped out by Indian raids, over and over, only to be revived and come to life again. It probably reached its peak about 1859, after mines were opened nearby, and population boomed to 1000 making it Arizona's leading metropolis. March 3rd of that year the territory's first newspaper, *The Weekly Arizonian*, was published at Tubac — it was moved to Tucson a few months later. In the early 1860's, when the start of the Civil War caused withdrawal of all troops, Apaches wrote another obituary for the town. It never again regained its No. 1 ranking.

Today the site of old Tubac presidio is a State Park, with a museum of relics reflecting the town's up and down past. And the hamlet has come to life a ninth time as the habitat of artists, actors and sportsmen. The golf club is owned by a group of famous touring pros.

## NOGALES-NOGALES

You don't have to cross an ocean to visit a romantic foreign country — just cross the street in Nogales, Arizona. A wire fence runs down the middle of the street, north of the fence is the United States, south is Mexico. Nogales, Sonora, population 50,000, is several times larger than Nogales, Arizona, but citizens of the two communities like to think of them as a single city which they call, "Ambos Nogales" (Both Nogales). Passage between them is through the arches of the modernistic International Gateway. No travel permits are required for brief trips into the Sonora city to shop, dine or attend the bullfights, which are held every Sunday. A long time favorite eating place across

the border is famous La Caverna, "The Cavern", a cave originally hollowed out of solid rock to serve as a jail. Tourists love to shop along Avenida Obregon for fabrics, serapes, silver jewelry, tooled leather, ceramics, and other popular Mexican merchandise.

Longer trips over excellent highways to Sonora's capital, Hermosillo, and to fascinating cities of Mexico's West Coast, may be arranged with a minimum of red tape. Travel Agencies, chambers of commerce, and Mexican consular officials will be glad to help and advise you. The friendly people of Sonora welcome visitors. The Mexican government maintains a "Friendly Fleet" of radio controlled cars which patrol the highways to provide assistance, free of charge, to tourists — everything from first aid to minor auto repairs, with gas, oil, and spare parts supplied at cost. How's THAT for hospitality? First class public transportation, air, rail and bus, is available, as are fine modern accommodations in the principal cities. In the gulf ports there's deep sea fishing, or you may take a 200-mile trip along the "Kino Mission Trail" to a number of missions in Sonora founded by the famous padre.

From Nogales U.S. 89 leads north, 18 miles to Tumacacori Mission, 66 miles to Tucson.

## SAN XAVIER MISSION

Perhaps the most beautiful of all the old Spanish missions, San Xavier del Bac, "White Dove of the Desert", is located nine miles south of Tucson. Padre Kino selected the site at the Indian village of Bac in 1700, but the original mission buildings were destroyed in the Pima revolt in 1751. The present building, completed in 1797 by the Franciscans, took 20 years to construct. Two snow white towers are separated by a central facade, weathered to a contrasting buff tone, and decorated with Spanish ornamentation. 'Tis said the second tower was purposely left unfinished to avoid the heavy Spanish tax on "finished" church structures.

Following Mexico's war of independence the mission was abandoned until the land became part of the United States after the Gadsen Purchase. Today the ancient edifice has been restored and is in active use as a church serving the Indians. There is no charge to visitors, but the mission is kept in repair only through voluntary contributions.

# TUCSON

One of the "ranches" that Padre Kino established near San Xavier Mission was at the little Pima village of "Stjukshon" (dark spring), which we know today as Tucson (too-sahn). Since 1691 the "Old Pueblo" has grown some, and has witnessed every phase of White Man's conquest of the Southwest. In 1776 the Spanish presidio was moved from Tubac to Tucson, and it became a walled city — the only walled city that the United States has ever known. For almost a century it was a sort of "ghetto", in which Apaches confined the "pale faces" — and woe be it to those they caught alone outside the wall.

In 1854, after the Gadsen Purchase, U.S. Dragoons took over protection of Tucson, and settlers started coming through in greater numbers than even the Apaches could handle. When the stages started regular schedules three years later, Tucson became a principal stop, and one of the toughest towns on the frontier.

Then came the Civil War. The troops marched away, and the stages stopped running. Naturally the Apaches thought they had won the war. Air pollution from their smoke signals covered Arizona, and people with hair had more to worry about than a hippie in a Marine boot camp barber chair. In February, 1862, Jefferson Davis proclaimed Arizona a territory of the Confederacy, and a troop of Texas cavalry occupied Tucson. Three months later, after a brief skirmish with California Volunteers, the troop rode back to Texas, and the Union column moved into Tucson, and its commander proclaimed Arizona a U.S. territory, thereby scooping Congress by more than a year. The

Apaches remained neutral — they shot soldiers regardless of the color of their uniforms.

The war was still on when Arizona attained its status as a territory in 1863. Since Tucson was generally reputed to be a hotbed of Southern sympathizers, Lincoln-appointed officials were not about to locate the seat of government here. By 1867, however, the legislature did move the capital to Tucson, where it remained for a decade before being returned to Prescott, and eventually to Phoenix.

After the Civil War, Tucson quickly outgrew its old Spanish wall, spilling out over the landscape, and crumbling the wall in the process. Mines were booming, word of Tucson's healthful climate spread rapidly through the land, and, in 1881, the railroad came to Tucson. In '87 ground was broken for the University of Arizona, located in Tucson to mollify the town for loss of the capital. Today Tucson is a leading metropolis of the Southwest, Arizona's second largest city. There is one tiny segment of the old TOWN WALL remaining, which you can see on the grounds of the County Courthouse.

The University of Arizona has grown until, if it were an incorporated municipality, its population would place it among the state's 10 top cities. It was at the UofA that Dr. Andrew Ellicott Douglass developed his famous TREE-RING SYSTEM, most accurate of all techniques for dating ancient events. Now this university is one of the few in the world employing the advanced ARCHEOMAGNETIC dating technique. (Undergrads employ the old traditional dating techniques.) When you visit the UofA campus be sure to see the ARIZONA STATE MUSEUM. Featured are exhibits and dioramas tracing life in this region back more than 11 centuries. There are scale models of Arizona's principal prehistoric ruins.

The beautiful desert around Tucson is filled with resorts and dude ranches. Inevitably, there are a number of fine golf courses from which

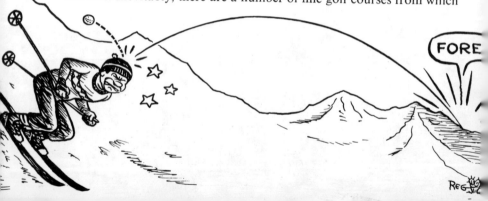

FORE

"sun worshippers" can plainly see snow on the Catalinas, where skiers frolic 35 miles away and a mile above, on MT. LEMMON, which doubles as a summer retreat in season.

Don't leave Tucson without visiting the ARIZONA-SONORA DESERT MUSEUM, located in a luxurient cactus forest, 15 miles west of town. Exhibits feature both plant and animal life of the Southwest. You'll mingle with birds in walk-through aviaries; you'll come face to face with bears, coyotes, javalinas and children may handle big desert tortoises. To us the most exciting exhibits at the Desert Museum are in the darkened tunnel, where you can switch on hidden lights and spy through windows into the underground dens of foxes, badgers, prairie dogs, porcupines, bats, and even rattlesnakes. In case the kids insist on making a day of it, there's a restaurant at the museum. Only a mile beyond the Desert Museum is the entrance to the land of giants.

# SAGUARO NATIONAL MONUMENT

The saguaro, monarch of Arizona's desert (see pages 67-68) is preserved in this National Monument, totaling 123 square miles, divided in two sections, equidistant, east and west of Tucson. The western part, near the Desert Museum, is the Tucson Mountain Section, newest area, in which the saguaros are also the "newest", a particularly fine stand of vigorous young giants, as well as a great variety of other desert plants. Picnic areas, with tables and restrooms are available here.

The older, original portion of Saguaro National Monument is 16 miles east of Tucson, and is a fully developed park containing mountains as well as desert. The Visitor Center has exhibits explaining how life adapts to the arid country, and high windows through which you can watch animals attracted to a waterhole outside. There's a nine-mile loop drive through the "Cactus Forest", populated by venerable giants, with parking spots and short trails where you can get out and walk 'mongst the goliaths. More than 50 miles of trails are provided for

Y'SEE SOME FUNNY LOOKIN' CRITTERS DOWN HERE!

serious hikers (check with the park ranger).

South of the Monument, 27 miles southeast of Tucson via Interstate 10, is a subterranean tourist attraction.

## COLOSSAL CAVE

They say about the rarest thing in the world is a dry cave, but this is one of them. There's not a trace of the great underground river which hollowed out the countless chambers, nor of the lime-laden dripping springs which built the cave's many columns, stalactites and stalagmites. One such formation is the Elephant's Head, realistic enough to bring joy to the heart of any Republican. Legend has it the pore critter took refuge here during early days of Arizona's statehood, and turned to stone before the state elected its first GOP legislature in 1966.

Back in the 1880's Colossal Cave was known only to outlaws, who used it as a hideout. To this day nobody knows exactly how "colossal" it is, for, though at least 40 miles of passages have been traced, it has never been completely explored. Operated as a county park, an hour-long tour is conducted through the cavern, over paved, electrically lighted walks and stairways.

After you have peered into Arizona's cavernous innards, you can study its matchless skies from a mountaintop on the Papago Indian Reservation, 53 miles southwest of Tucson.

## KITT PEAK

When astronomers first approached Papago tribal leaders for permission to establish a great observatory on their Kitt Peak, they were not favorably impressed. The idea of peeking into the heavens from the sacred mountain sounded like "bad medicine". Then they were invited to the UofA campus for a look through Steward Observatory's 36-inch reflecting telescope. What they saw changed their minds, and they agreed to lease the high ground to the "men with the long eyes".

THAT REMINDS ME – I OUGHTA HAVE TH' DENTIST CHECK MY MOLARS!

Today America's most advanced astronomical complex occupies the 200-acre site, and the Indians are among its most ardent supporters. The 36-inch Steward Observatory telescope has been moved up there, away from the city lights, and the UofA has built another 90-inch telescope to augment it. But the mountain has many eyes, and these are but two of them. The principal installations are those of the Kitt Peak National Observatory, operated by the Associated Universities (California, Chicago, Michigan, Wisconsin, Harvard, Indiana, Ohio State, Princeton, and Yale) for the National Science Foundation. Everywhere you look are glistening silver domes, each housing a telescope, with more and bigger ones to come. The structure that dominates all the others is one that looks like Picasso had started to sculp an enormous letter "N", and left off one of the uprights. This is the Robert McMath Solar Telescope. The slanting part of the "N" extends deep into the ground, and is a 480-foot shaft, exactly parallel to the earth's axis. An 80-inch mirror at the top follows the sun and relays its beams to the bottom of the shaft. In the underground observing room they keep tabs on old Sol, its nuclear flareups, rays and spots, photographing and spectroscoping every mood. When we start regular travel in space, it's going to be a matter of life and death to know all about the planets and stars, particularly the sun-star we're hitched to. At Kitt Peak they're working on the answers.

**STARS DON'T HAVE ANY PRIVACY ANY MORE!**

Visitors are welcome at the National Observatory, which is open daily, from 10 a.m. 'til 4 p.m. — no charge. Turn off Rte. 86 about 40 miles west of Tucson, and drive 12 miles south on the fine highway which soars to the Peak. A dozen and a half miles west of the Kitt Peak turnoff is Sells, the Papago agency town and tribal capital.

## THE PAPAGOS

In the 130-mile stretch of Rte. 86 between Tucson and Ajo, 100 miles is across the vast 2,800,000-acre Papago Reservation, through

desert which looks about like it did when the Spaniard, Melchior Diaz, journeyed this way in 1540. It's a kind of lonesome road, paved, but not heavily traveled, and purposely laid out to bypass many small villages. This reduces traffic hazards for the Indians, and gives them a measure of privacy. Not that the Papagos are unfriendly, they just don't fancy themselves as "tourist attractions". The men dress more like cowboys than the TV-type "redskins". In fact, these Indians were cowboys before the Texas-style buckaroos arrived in Arizona. They learned the cattle raising business from the Spanish missionaries centuries ago. One of the few reservation events open to the public is the annual Papago Rodeo in the fall. Another public affair is the Feast of St. Francis, a ceremonial which reflects the influence of the old padres, with its mass, feasting, dancing, games and fireworks. It is held each October in Sells.

Throughout their history, the Papagos have made use of desert-plant fibers, fruit and seeds for food, beverages, baskets, mats, clothing and for building materials. You'll still see traditional dwellings made with saguaro poles, desert brush, yucca leaves, plastered with mud, but more and more modern housing is coming into use. At the trading posts look for the fine Papago baskets, made from yucca leaves, with designs produced from strands of the devil's claw pod, one of nature's rarities — a true black. Sometimes the baskets are a little hard to come by, since the women now produce them on a sort of spare-time basis.

One of the greatest national cactus preserves is adjacent to the Papago Reservation, on the west, along the Mexican border.

## ORGAN PIPE CACTUS

A long time ago, before this part of Arizona was in the United States, two tribes from Sonora infiltrated the desert south of Ajo. When Mexico and the U.S. established the international boundary, these "Mexicans" could not move back across the line, because they had put down roots — literally. They were cactus-plant "tribes" — a colony of *organ pipe* cacti, and a small band of *senita* "old man",

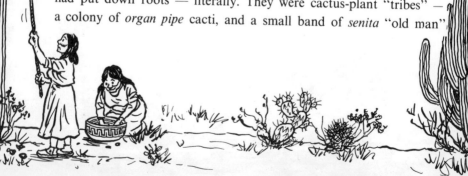

cacti. In Mexico both varieties grow in profusion, but this "invasion" area is the only part of the U.S. where they may be seen outside a cactus garden. A 500-square-mile section along the border has been set aside, named the Organ Pipe Cactus National Monument, to guarantee a permanent home for the "infiltrators".

We've described the organ pipe cactus on page 68. The senita is a similarly constructed cereus plant, but it is smaller, with fewer, deeper ribs and grooves. At the tops of its older branches the spines turn into matted white bristles, that look like gray hair — which gives it the name of senita, for "senile" old man.

Be sure to stop at the Visitor Center, 17 miles south of the Monument entrance, to get information before driving or hiking through this wild and unspoiled desert landscape. There are two graded loop-trips, the 21-mile Ajo Mountain Drive, and the 51-mile Puerto Blanco Drive, and side roads like the one to Senità Basin, where the "old men" live.

Lukeville, on the Mexican border, is only five miles south of the Visitor Center. You can drive across the line for lunch or dinner, in Sonoita, Sonora. Sonoita is the gateway to deep sea fishing in the Gulf of California, only 66 miles away, via Mexico Highway 8, at Puerto Penasco (Rocky Point), which has become enormously popular with Arizona sportsmen.

## BOMBS AND GARLIC

You arrive at the Organ Pipe Visitor Center by driving 32 miles south on Rte. 85 from Ajo, and you arrive at Ajo via Rte. 86 from Tucson, or by turning off Interstate 8 at Gila Bend (once a Butterfield Stage stop), and driving south 42 miles. This stretch of highway between Gila Bend and Ajo crosses an enormous and very active Air Force Bombing and Gunnery Range. DO NOT wander off the right-of-way of this road, unless you'd like to become a moving target.

HAVE YOU HEARD OF THE TOWN NAMED AFTER GARLIC?

Ajo (AH-hoe) is Spanish for "garlic". The town was named for the wild garlic plants that pioneers found growing all over the nearby hills. Ajo is one of the state's oldest mining towns, where digging has been continuous for well over a century. The first ore was packed out of here to Yuma on mule back, in the 1880's, at a cost of $105 per ton. Today the New Cornelia at Ajo is one of Arizona's biggest open pit mines, and close by is the great $7 million smelter. A public lookout point provides a breathtaking view of the man-made chasm.

Forty miles northwest of Tucson on Interstate 10, is Picacho State Park.

# TEXAS 3, CALIFORNIA 2

Picacho Peak has a silhouette which, from the highway, looks like the head of a coyote, tilted skyward, yelping at the moon. It was in the pass at the base of this peak that Arizona's only Civil War battle was fought, April 15, 1862. A scouting party of 16 Confederates from Texas, commanded by Lt. Jack Swilling (who later founded Phoenix) tangled with a dozen advance guards from the California Column. To the three Union and two Confederate soldiers who died here, it was the biggest battle of the war — to history it was the westernmost skirmish of the conflict. To the Texans it was a turning point — they turned 'round and headed back to Texas, satisfied to settle for a 3-2 "win" over California. As for Lt. Swilling, he decided to give up his military career and go into prospecting.

Halfway between Tucson and Phoenix is the valley of the Big Houses.

# CASA GRANDE VALLEY

In Spanish Casa Grande (cah-sah GRAHN-day) means "big house". It was the name given the now famous prehistoric ruins by Padre Kino when he discovered them in 1694. Arizona's other kind

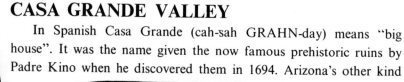

of "big house", the state prison, is also in the Valley, near Florence, a town which prefers to be known as the birthplace of the "junior rodeo", staged for fledgling buckaroos each November, and widely imitated throughout the West. Most scenic approach to Casa Grande Valley is by way of the Pinal Pioneer Parkway to Florence, the faster freeway route is Interstate 10, via Picacho and Eloy.

The town of Casa Grande, largest in the Valley, is not the site of the ruin, it's the training center for the San Francisco Giants baseball organization, where winter visitors come to watch the big leaguers get into shape, and where hundreds of younger players are brought to train, compete, and try out for the majors.

Coolidge is only two miles from America's first high-rise apartment house.

## CASA GRANDE RUINS

We hasten to point out that the great roof, held aloft by four slanting steel columns, which is the first thing you see above the landscape as you approach Casa Grande Ruins, was erected by the National Park Service, not prehistoric Indians. Each of those four columns is set in a 68-ton block of concrete, not only to hold the roof up, but to hold it down when the gusty desert winds blow. The roof shelters the highest section of Casa Grande Ruins National Monument to keep it from melting into another earthen mound under the onslaught of the elements. When Padre Kino first saw the ruins they were already 700 years old, but still quite well preserved. By the time they were taken under the wing of the Park Service, 200 years later, the Casa was eroding away at an alarming rate.

Today, even in ruin, it is impressive, a four-story tower with walls

four feet thick at the base. The walls are not made of adobe brick, but of solid mud, the prehistoric equivalent of poured concrete. This "skyscraper" did double duty as a dwelling and as a lookout for the village, which housed hundreds of farmers. The horse had not yet arrived in America, so enemy raiders, approaching on foot, could be spotted in plenty of time to warn workers in the field.

The Hohokam had been irrigating and farming this valley for centuries, when the Pueblo Indians, driven south by the big drouth of the 1200s, pushed into Central Arizona. The two cultures blended, and Casa Grande reflects the Pueblo influence on Hohokam architecture. Many have wondered what happened to the vanished people who built these ancient villages and their vast irrigation systems. Dr. Emil Haury, of the UofA, thinks "they're still here" on the Gila River Indian Reservation.

## PIMA INDIANS

Dr. Haury's excavations have indicated that the Hohokam pottery, agriculture, and way of life were very similar to that of the early Pimas. He believes they are the direct descendants of the ancient people. The Pimas of today are still master farmers, but now instead of stone hoes, they work their land with the most modern of agricultural machinery. Their water comes from Coolidge Dam through very modern canals, but some of these follow the old channels laid out by their ancestors.

Since the beginning of White Man's history in the Southwest, the Pimas have been his friends. The Pima Villages were looked upon as havens of safety by the pioneers. Their reservation, in the Casa Grande Valley, with its agency at Sacaton, was the first in Arizona, established by Congress in 1859. You will find them a friendly people today.

# HELL AND/OR HEAVEN

For centuries summertime in Yuma had a thermal rating which could be, and frequently was compared to the Nether Regions. Yuma became synonymous with "heat", since weather reports frequently listed it as the nation's hottest spot. But modern air conditioning has taken the devil out of Yuma's summers. Today, though outside temperatures, June to October, can be hellish (as in most of central and southern Arizona), all indoors is refrigerated, so you can "keep your cool" at home, in the stores, offices, hotels, or in your car. And, of course, now as always, the winters are heavenly.

Ever since Hernando de Alarcon discovered the site in 1540, Yuma has been famous as a crossing place between Arizona and California. Spaniards forded the Colorado River here for more than 240 years. And, when gold was discovered at Sutter's Mill, enterprising Americans established a ferry at the old Spanish crossing to handle the gold rushers. More than 60,000 crossed in 1850-51. It was here that the "Jackass Mail" and Butterfield stages made regular crossings.

Fort Yuma was established in '51, on the California side of the Colorado, but the little river port which sprang up on the Arizona side, was first called Colorado City, then Arizona City, before finally being named Yuma. Life on the banks of the stream was not recommended for folks with jumpy nerves. At flood time Big Red, with its towering "sand waves", was an uncontrollable terror. At least twice it swept away the whole town.

In 1877 the Southern Pacific railroad arrived across the river from Yuma, where the government granted permission to build a bridge. But, when it was finished, permission for trains to cross was refused

YUMA
TERRITORIAL
PRISON

GUARD HOUSE
CELL BLOCK

till fighting between competing RR builders could be settled. Arizona's first full sized locomotive came to the territory in a "sneak preview", when the train crew illegally ran their engine 'cross the bridge at midnight, Sept. 29. It was 1878 before an act of Congress and a territorial charter permitted the railroad to lay tracks across Arizona.

In the early 1900s an automobile arrived at the river and was ferried across. Then another, and another. By 1915 there was a steady stream — a car a day. So the first steel traffic bridge was built. Today's modern bridge carries more than 6000 cars and trucks per day.

Today no steamboats ply the Colorado, but all kinds of motor craft, some towing water skiers, churn the now blue waters of the main channel, while fishing boats float contentedly in the backwater lagoons. North of Yuma 46,000 acres have been set aside in the Imperial National Wildlife Refuge, nesting place for snowy egrets, and great blue herons, and a favorite gathering place for 195 other bird species. In this area, a short drive from Yuma, is Imperial Dam, and above it Lake Martinez, a popular recreation spot.

South of Yuma, through the nearby Mexican border town of San Luis, is the Gulf of California, one of the world's greatest deep sea fishing grounds.

Reformed old Colorado River makes a serious, as well as recreational, contribution to Yuma's economy. Its waters are siphoned off to irrigate a 200,000-acre agricultural empire in Yuma and Gila Valleys, Yuma Mesa, and in Wellton-Mohawk Valley to the east.

There's no irrigation nor refrigeration in the million-acre Army Proving Grounds, 25 miles northeast of Yuma, where men and mili-

tary equipment are tested under extremes of heat. On the outskirts of Yuma is the Marine Corps Auxiliary Air Station, where Leathernecks are trained in the art of jet flying. They even have a "carrier deck" marked out on the desert, to practice really "dry runs".

One building which never enjoyed air conditioning, became the official home of some of Arizona's worst bad men.

## THE TERRITORIAL PRISON

On a bluff overlooking the junction of the Gila and Colorado Rivers, near the bridges in downtown Yuma, is the ruin of Arizona's old "bastille", which opened for business July 1, 1876, with seven tenants. Of the 104 convicts buried in the prison graveyard, more than half died trying to escape. In 33 years only one ever succeeded. The prison was moved to Florence in 1909.

Today the old penitentiary is a State Park and museum. You may peer into the cell blocks, through the arched doors, secured by flat iron bars. Most of the walls are made of thick 'dobe, though some cells are hollowed out of solid rock in the bluff. All were built by the convicts themselves — the most printable name they ever called the prison was "Hell-Hole".

And now, we'd like to walk with you into the darkest cell. What more fitting place to end a sentence than in a prison? So that's where we'll put a period to this brief tour of Arizona — and that's where we'll leave you now — in the dungeon of Yuma's old Territorial Prison.

## ADIOS!

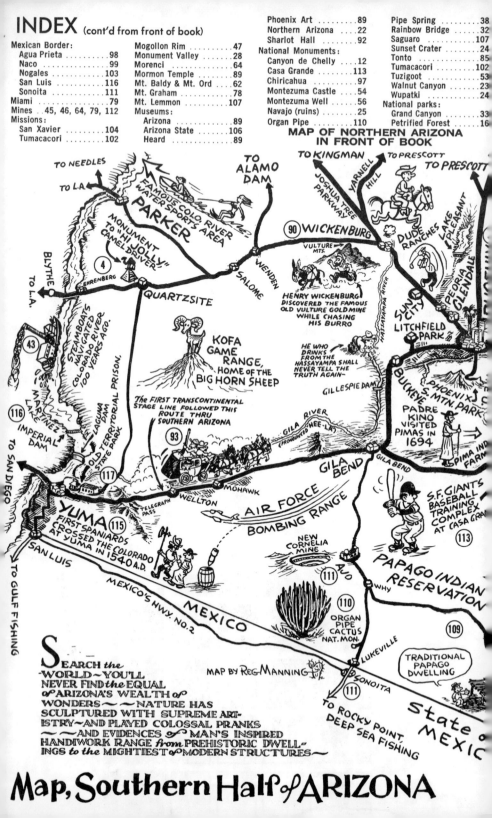

# INDEX (cont'd from front of book)

MAP OF NORTHERN ARIZONA IN FRONT OF BOOK

# Map, Southern Half of ARIZONA

## Numbers in circles on map refer to pages in the text.

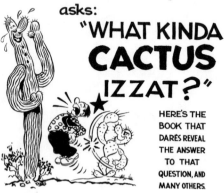